Betty's Poems

❦

Compiled by
Betty M. Grant

Library of Congress Number:		2005907638
ISBN:	Hardcover	1-59926-538-9
	Softcover	1-59926-537-0

To order additional copies of this book, contact:
Xlibris Corporation
1-888-795-4274
www.Xlibris.com
Orders@Xlibris.com
25901

Contents

Preface And Acknowledgements 13

List Of Illustrations 17

I Remember, I Remember 19

Memory 21

In Flander's Field 24

In Kentucky 25

Motherhood 27

Somebody's Mother 29

Which Loved Best? 31

In School Days 32

Lifting And Leaning 35

The Man With The Hoe 36

The Reading Mother 38

Hugs 40

Where Did You Come From 42

Samantha's Poems 44

People 44

Mother Nature 45

The Sky Is Pink 45

I Have A Different Shadow 46

Flying Love 46

Attachment 48

Little Things 48

Give me a good digestion, Lord 49

My Influence 50

Commit thy works unto the Lord..50

So teach us to number our days 50

Go thy way; as thou hast believed 50

The Children's Hour 51

The Swing 54

Formula for youth 55

Growing old is only a bad habit 55

May you live all the days..55

Those attributes which keep the mind young 55

Hiawatha's Childhood 56

My Shadow 59

The Bear Story 60

The Rainbow 64

Griggsby's Station 65

The Raggedy Man 68

Out To Old Aunt Mary's..71

Little Orphant Annie 76

Think About The Lovely Things 79

Wynken, Blynken, And Nod 80

The Duel 82

New Friends And Old Friends 85

Do Not Find Fault 86

Our Own 87

A Creed For Later Years 88

Stone walls do not a prison make 89

Three Gates 90

Man's capacity for justice 90

Charity 91

Say It Now..91

The Bridge Builder 92

At The Place Of The Sea...93

I Said A Prayer For You Today 94

My flesh and heart faileth 95

Rejoicing in hope; patient in tribulation 95
Casting all your care upon him 95
For I am thy God, I will strengthen thee 95
You Encouraged Me 96
Poems 97
Touch Hands 98
One immediate fruit of patience is peace 99
She Dwelt Among The Untrodden Ways 100
Sweet Peril 101
Oh Let My Love 102
All Paths Lead To You 103
There Are Such Things 105
I just kissed your picture good-night 105
Only We 106
A Woman's Question 108
But don't be afraid that distance 109
The Heart Of A Girl Is A Wonderful Thing 110
Maud Muller 112
The Courtin' 117
Ten Commandments For Husbands 121
Ten Commandments For Wives 123
The Fiftieth Anniversary 125
A Red, Red Rose 128
In Your Arms 129
I Look To Thee In Every Need 131
Simple Things 131
Work is what you have to do 131
Growing Old 132
Touching Shoulders 133
The Tiger 134
An Old Sweetheart Of Mine 136
Light Shining Out Of Darkness 140
How The Great Guest Came 141

A Creed 143

The Winds Of Fate 144

An Evening Prayer 145

Man Was Made To Mourn 146

He Who Knows 147

Retribution 148

Though the mills of God grind slowly 148

The Touch Of The Master's Hand............................ 149

More things are wrought by prayer 150

Abou Ben Adhem 151

The Lord is my shepherd, I shall not want................ 152

I Know Not What The Future 153

Prayer For Those Who Live Alone 154

Thanatopsis 155

If we have been joined to Him 155

Crossing The Bar 156

Death!.. 157

There hath not failed one word................................ 158

Jesus said, "Lo, I am with you always"..................... 158

I will never leave thee or forsake thee 158

To A Waterfowl 159

The quality of mercy is not strained 160

Meekness is humility.. 161

Yesterday is already a dream.................................... 161

The Guy In The Glass 162

What God Hath Promised 163

My Moment With God 164

He that dwelleth in the secret place of the most High 165

Preaching Vs Living 167

The love of reading enables a man............................ 168

A wise man will hear and increase learning.............. 168

Good Morning God 169

Only Believe 170

The Road Not Taken 171
If of thy mortal goods thou are bereft 172
Pleasure And Sorrow 173
Life's Tapestry 174
As A Fond Mother 175
God shall be my hope 176
Life gives us blessings without end 176
God give you strength for all your needs 176
These Are The Gifts I Ask 177
Myself 178
The Day Is Done 179
The Human Touch 180
Outwitted 180
October's Bright Blue Weather 181
But as for me, I trust in you 183
The meek will he guide in judgment 183
In thee oh Lord, do I put my trust 183
As it is written, eye hath not seen 183
The earth is full of the loving kindness 183
All Things Bright And Beautiful 184
Barefoot Boy 185
The Sandpiper 187
Old October 189
To My Dear And Loving Husband 191
The Old Swimmin'-Hole 193
Jenny Kiss'd Me 195
Trees 196
When The Frost Is On The Punkin 197
Daffodils 199
The First Snowfall 200
The Bridge 202
If I can stop one heart from breaking 204
The Beautiful Life 205

The Year's At The Spring 206

Our Lips And Ears 206

A Backward Look 207

The House By The Side Of The Road 209

Do Not Go Gentle Into That Good Night 211

Elegy In A Country Church Yard 212

To A Louse 218

A Wise Old Owl 218

O Captain! My Captain! 219

Index of Authors 221

Dedication

In memory of my mother,
Dinksie Lake Robinson

Preface And Acknowledgements

I have always had a love of poetry. This is due in a large measure, I believe, to the influence of my mother who was a poet at heart and often said she envied poets. She taught my brothers and me to read all literature, especially poetry. From my earliest childhood, as we would share household chores, she often recited stories and poems recalled from her school teaching days. She was blessed with a good memory and could quote long passages from her favorite poems.

I learned at an early age that poetry is not only entertaining, but, in time of need, gives comfort to the reader. It brings back memories and scenes from the distant past and satisfies our hunger for beauty and truth in ways that prose can never achieve, even in its most eloquent manner.

I have collected poetry lifelong. Poems having a special appeal were clipped from newspapers and magazines or copied in notebooks or, occasionally, on scraps of paper. Through the years, the quantity grew to a large number, which were kept, unorganized, in various locations in our home. When Fred, my husband, suggested we compile them into a collection, I was pleased and excited.

When Fred and I became acquainted, poetry played a part in the growth of our friendship and in the love that developed. Poetry has added to the strength and beauty of our marriage.

It is only in recent years that I have begun to fully understand and appreciate the rich legacy my mother gave by introducing me to the beauty and power of poetry. I followed her example by reading and teaching literature to our children beginning when they were infants. I am pleased they continued this practice with our grandchildren.

When I was young, almost every issue of popular magazines and newspapers contained one or more poems. I am sad that this is no longer true and that there is little poetry on radio or television. It is gratifying, however, to find that there are several excellent websites on the Internet that contain poetry and promote the reading of it. Nevertheless, I am unhappy to read that interest in all reading has declined in recent years.

For many years, my husband and I were involved in a number of book discussion groups. We were disappointed to discover that few of the members enjoyed or understood poetry. I have read that a mere 15% of the population read poetry today. By publishing poems I have loved and grown up with, I hope that in some small incremental measure the reading of poetry will be promoted.

As every person who reads, I owe a debt of gratitude to the endless legion of writers of poetry who have shared their innermost thoughts and emotions from the earliest days of recorded history. From before Christ, poets have expressed the thoughts and deepest emotions of humankind and have brought pleasure to generations of readers. We have a much better understanding of historical events because of the vast riches of poetry. Without those gifts, our knowledge of our ancestors would be lacking in many ways.

The majority of the poems in this collection were penned and published in the 19th century, the golden age of poetry, which places them in the public domain. Nevertheless, every effort has been made to trace possible copyright ownerships of each poem through the Library of Congress Copyright Catalog, The New York City Public Library copyright data, local libraries, and WATCH. Several letters requesting permission were mailed to individuals and publishers. It is sincerely regretted if there is a question regarding the use of any material without permission. In the event of such an error, it is entirely unintentional.

Grateful acknowledgement is made to the New Directions Publishing Corporation for giving permission to reproduce Do Not Go Gentle Into That Good Night by Dylan Thomas.

A special thanks to my friend and neighbor, Marian Wiese, an artist, and our daughter Laura Altevers, for the several drawings they contributed to illustrate poems in this book. Laura also provided invaluable assistance in formatting the book for submittal to the publisher.

I am grateful for the assistance and encouragement provided by our daughter Janey Kennedy and our son John. I also appreciate the support from my husband, Fred, in arriving at the decision to publish my collection and for entering the poems into a word processing program.

Betty Marie Grant

June 2005

List Of Illustrations

Page   **Illustration and Poem**

20   Birthplace—*I Remember, I Remember*
23   Abraham Lincoln and son Tad—*Memory*
26   "Maiden's eyes are the bluest" (Betty's
           granddaughters)—*In Kentucky*
34   Scaffold Cane School—*School Days*
39   Betty Grant, 1970—*A Reading Mother*
41   Janey and Johnny Grant, 1948—*Hugs*
43   Betty and granddaughter Samantha—*Where Did You Come
           From?*
47   Samantha Schultz—*Samantha's Poems*
53   "In the round tower of my heart" (Betty's children)—*The
           Children's Hour*
67   Haynes Homestead in western Oklahoma—*Griggsby's
           Station*
75   Home of John and Jan Grant—*Out To Old Aunt Mary's*
84   Gingham Dog & Calico Cat (L. Altevers)—*The Duel*
92   The Bridge—*The Bridge Builder*
104   Betty and Fred Grant—*All Paths Lead To You*
107   "Eye to Eye" (Betty and Fred)—*Only We*
111   "The heart of a girl" (Betty as a young woman)—*The Heart
           Of A Girl Is A Wonderful Thing*
117   Silhouette—*The Courtin'*
127   Betty and Fred Grant—*The Fiftieth Anniversary*
130   Jeremy Grant—*In Your Arms*
135   Tiger, Tiger (L. Altevers)—*The Tiger*
144   Sailing Ship—*The Winds Of Fate*
159   Waterfowl (M. Wiese)—*To A Waterfowl*
166   Dinksie Lake Robinson—*My Moment With God*

172   Hyacinths—*Persian Proverb*
186   Fred Grant—*The Barefoot Boy*
188   Sandpipers (M. Wiese)—*The Sandpiper*
192   "If ever two were one" (Betty and Fred)—*To My Dear And Loving Husband*
196   The Tree (M. Wiese)—*Trees*
118   The Pumpkin (M. Wiese)—*When The Frost Is On The Punkin*
210   Home of John W. Lakes—*The House By The Side Of The Road*
217   Highland Cemetery, Highland County, Ohio—*Elegy In A Country Churchyard*

I Remember, I Remember

I remember, I remember,
The house where I was born,
The little window where the sun
Came peeping in at morn;
He never came a wink too soon,
Nor brought too long a day,
But now, I often wish the night
Had borne my breath away.

I remember, I remember,
The roses, red and white;
The violets and the lily-cups,
Those flowers made of light!
The lilacs where the robin built,
And where my brother set
The laburnum on his birthday—
The tree is living yet!

I remember, I remember,
Where I used to swing;
And thought the air must rush as fresh
To swallows on the wing:
My spirit flew in feathers then,
That is so heavy now,
And summer pools could hardly cool
The fever on my brow!

I remember, I remember,
The fir trees dark and high;
I used to think their slender tops
Were close against the sky;
It was a childish ignorance,
But now 'tis little joy
To know I'm farther off from heaven
Than when I was a boy.

Thomas Hood

"I remember, I remember, the house where I was born"

The house where Betty Robinson Grant
was born, near Berea, Kentucky

Memory

My childhood home I see again,
And sadden with the view;
And still, as memory crowds my brain,
There's pleasure in it, too.

O memory! Thou midway world
'Twixt earth and paradise,
Where things decayed and loved ones lost
In dreamy shadows rise.

And, freed from all that's earthly, vile,
Seen hallowed, pure and bright,
Like scenes in some enchanted isle
All bathed in liquid light.

As dusky mountains please the eye
Where twilight chases day;
As bugle notes that, passing by,
In distance die away;

As leaving some grand waterfall,
We, lingering, list its roar—
So memory will hallow all
We've known, but know no more.

Near twenty years have passed away
Since here I bid farewell
To woods and fields, and scenes of play,
And playmates loved so well.

Where many were, but few remain
Of old familiar things,
But seeing them, to mind again
The lost and absent brings.

The friends I left that parting day,
How changed as time has sped!
Young childhood grown, strong manhood gray,
And half of all are dead.

I hear the loved survivors tell
How nought from death could save,
Till every sound appears a knell
And every spot a grave.

I range the fields with pensive tread,
And pace the hollow rooms,
And feel (companion of the dead)
I'm living in the tombs.

Abraham Lincoln
(Written at the age of 37)

Abraham Lincoln with his son Tad

In Flander's Field

In Flander's Field the poppies blow
Between the crosses, row on row,
That mark our place, and in the sky
The larks, still bravely singing, fly
Scarce heard amid the guns below.

We are the Dead. Short days ago
We lived, felt dawn, saw sunset glow,
Loved and were loved, and now we lie
In Flander's field.

Take up your quarrel with the foe;
To you from failing hands we throw
The torch; be yours to hold it high.
If ye break faith with us who die
We shall not sleep, though poppies grow
In Flanders Field

John McRae

In Kentucky

The moonlight falls the softest,
In Kentucky;
The summer days come oft'est,
In Kentucky;
Friendship is the strongest,
Love's fire glows the longest,
Yet, a wrong is always wrongest,
In Kentucky.

The sun shines ever brightest
In Kentucky;
The breezes whisper lightest
In Kentucky;
Plain girls are the fewest,
Maidens' eyes the bluest,
Their little hearts are the truest,
In Kentucky.

Life's burdens bear the lightest
In Kentucky;
The home fires burn the brightest
In Kentucky.
While players are the keenest,
Cards come out the meanest,
The pocket empties cleanest,
In Kentucky.

The songbirds are the sweetest
In Kentucky;
The thoroughbreds the fleetest
In Kentucky;
Mountains tower proudest,
Thunder peals the loudest,
The landscape is the grandest—
And politics—the damnedest,
In Kentucky

James H. Mulligan

"Maidens' eyes the bluest"

*Betty's blue-eyed granddaughters,
(left to right) Erin and Laura Kennedy,
Samantha Schultz*

Motherhood

Mary, the Christ long slain, passed silently,
Following the children joyously astir
Under the cedrus and the olive tree,
Pausing to let their laughter float to her—
Each voice an echo of a voice more dear,
She saw a little Christ in every face.

When lo, another woman gliding near
Yearned o'er the tender life which filled the place.
And Mary sought the woman's hand, and spoke:
"I know thee not, yet know thy memory tossed
With all a thousand dreams their eyes evoke
Who bring to thee a child beloved and lost.

"I, too, have rocked my Little One.
And He was fair!
Oh, fairer than the fairest sun,
And, like its rays through amber spun,
His sun-bright hair.
Still I can see it shine and shine."
"Even so," the woman said, "was mine."
"His ways were ever darling ways"—

And Mary smiled—
"So soft, so clinging! Glad relays
Of love were all His precious days. My Little Child!
My infinite star! My music fled!"
"Even so was mine," the woman said.

And Mary whispered: "Tell me, thou,
Of thine." And she:
"Oh, mine was rosy as a bough
Blooming with roses, sent somehow,
To bloom for me!
His balmy fingers left a thrill
Deep in my breast that warms me still."

Then gazed she down some wilder, darker hour,
And said—when Mary questioned, knowing not:
"Who art thou, mother of so sweet a flower?"—
"I am the mother of Iscariot."

Agnes Lee

Somebody's Mother

The woman was old and ragged and gray
And bent with the chill of the Winter's day.

The street was wet with a recent snow
And the woman's feet were aged and slow.

She stood at the crossing and waited long,
Alone, uncared for, amid the throng

Of human beings who passed her by
Nor heeded the glance of her anxious eye.

Down the street, with laughter and shout,
Glad in the freedom of "school let out."

Came the boys like a flock of sheep,
Hailing the snow piled white and deep.

Past the woman so old and gray
Hastened the children on their way.

None offered a helping hand to her—
So meek, so timid, afraid to stir

Lest the carriage wheels or the horses' feet
Should crowd her down in the slippery street.

At last came one of the merry troop,
The gayest laddie of all the group;

He paused beside her and whispered low,
"I'll help you cross, if you wish to go."

Her aged hand on his strong young arm
She placed, and so, without hurt or harm,

He guided the trembling feet along,
Proud that his own were firm and strong.

Then back again to his friends he went,
His young heart happy and well content.

"She's somebody's mother, boys, you know,
For all she's aged and poor and slow,

"And I hope some fellow will lend a hand
To help my mother, you understand,

"If ever she's poor and old and gray,
When her own dear boy is far away."

And "somebody's mother" bowed her head
In her home that night, and the prayer she said

Was, "God be kind to the noble boy,
Who is somebody's son, and pride and joy!"

Mary Dow Brine

Which Loved Best?

"I love you Mother," said little John;
Then forgetting his work, his cap went on,
And he was off to the garden swing,
And left her the water and wood to bring.
"I love you Mother," said rosy Nell—
"I love you better than tongue can tell;"
Then she teased and pouted full half the day,
Till her mother rejoiced when she went out to play.
"I love you Mother," said little Fan;
"Today I'll help all I can;
How glad am I that school doesn't keep!"
So she rocked the baby until it fell asleep.

Then, stepping softly, she fetched the broom,
And swept the floor and tidied the room;
Busy and happy all day was she,
Helpful and happy as child could be.
"I love you Mother," again they said,
Three little children going to bed;
How do you think that mother guessed
Which one of them loved her the best?

Joy Allison

31

In School Days

Still sits the schoolhouse by the road.
A ragged beggar sunning;
Around it still the sumachs grow,
and blackberry vines are running.

Within, the master's desk is seen,
Deep scarred by raps official;
The warping floor, the battered seats,
The jackknife's carved initial;

The charcoal frescoes on its wall;
Its door's worn sill, betraying
The feet that, creeping slow to school,
Went storming out to playing!

Long years ago a winter sun
Shone over it at setting;
Lit up its western windowpanes,
And low eaves' icy fretting.

It touched the tangled golden curls,
And brown eyes full of grieving,
Of one who still her steps delay
When all the school were leaving.

For near her stood the little boy
Her childish favor singled;

His cap pulled low upon a face
Where pride and shame were mingled.

Pushing with restless feet the snow
To right and left he lingered;
As restlessly her tiny hands
The blue checked apron fingered.

He saw her lift her eyes; he felt
The soft hand's light caressing,
And heard the tremble of her voice,
As if a fault confessing.

"I'm sorry that I spelt the word;
I hate to go above you,
Because"—the brown eyes lower fell—
"Because, you see, I love you!"

Still memory to a gray-haired man
That sweet child-face is showing.
Dear girl! The grasses on her grave
Have forty years been growing!

He lives to learn, in life's hard school
How few who pass above him
Lament their triumph and his loss,
Like her—because they love him.

John Greenleaf Whittier

"In School Days"

Scaffold Cane School, Berea, Kentucky; 1931.
Betty is in the first row, second from left.

Lifting And Leaning

There are two kinds of people on earth today,
Just two kinds of people, no more, I say.

Not the good and the bad, for 'tis well understood
The good are half bad and the bad are half good.

Not the happy and sad, for the swift-flying years
Bring each man his laughter and each man his tears.

Not the rich and the poor, for to count a man's wealth
You must first know the state of his conscience and health.

Not the humble and proud, for in life's busy span
Who puts on vain airs is not counted a man.

No! the two kinds of people on earth I mean
Are the people who lift and the people who lean.

Wherever you go you will find the world's masses
Are ever divided in just these two classes.

And strangely enough, you will find, too, I ween,
There is only one lifter to twenty who lean.

In which class are you? Are you easing the load
Of overtaxed lifters who toil down the road?

Or are you a leaner who lets others bear
Your portion of worry, and labor and care?

Ella Wheeler Wilcox

The Man With The Hoe

(Written After Seeing the Painting by Millet)

God made man in His own image,
in the image of God made He him.
—Genesis 1:27

Bowed by the weight of centuries he leans
Upon his hoe and gazes at the ground,
The emptiness of ages in his face,
And upon his back the burden of the world.
Who made him dead to rapture and despair,
A thing that grieves not and that never hopes,
Stolid and stunned, a brother to the ox?
Who loosened and let down this brutal jaw?
Whose was the hand that slanted back the brow?
Whose breath blew out the light within this brain?

Is this the Thing the Lord God made and gave
To have dominion over sea and land
To trace the stars and search the heavens for power,
To feel the passion of Eternity?
Is this the Dream He dreamed who shaped the suns
And pillared the blue firmament with light?
Down all the stretch of hell to its last gulf
There is no shape more terrible than this—
More tongued with censure of the world's blind greed—
More filled with signs and portents for the soul—
More fraught with menace to the universe.

What gulfs between him and the seraphim!
Slaves of the wheel of labor, what to him
Are Plato and the swing of Pleiades?
What the long reaches of the peaks of song
The rift of dawn, the redding of the rose?
Through this dread shape the suffering ages look;
Time's tragedy is in that aching stoop,
Through this dread shape humanity betrayed,
Plundered, profaned, and disinherited,
Cries protest to the Judges of the World,
A protest that is also prophecy.

O masters, lords, and rulers in all lands,
Is this the handiwork you give to God,
This monstrous thing distorted and soul-quenched?
How will you ever straighten up this shape,
Touch it again with immortality;
Give back the upward looking and the light;
Rebuild in it the music and the dream;
Make right the immemorial infamies,
Perfidious wrongs, immedicable woes?

O masters, rulers, and lords in all lands,
How will the Future reckon with this Man?
How answer his brute question in that hour
When whirlwinds of rebellion shake the world?
How will it be with kingdoms and with kings—
With those who shaped him to the thing he is—
When this dumb Terror shall reply to God,
After the silence of the centuries?

Edwin Markham

The Reading Mother

I had a mother who read to me
Sagas of pirates who scoured the sea,
Cutlasses clinched in their yellow teeth,
"Blackbirds" stowed in the hold beneath.

I had a mother who read me lays;
Of ancient and gallant and golden days;
Stories of Marmion and Ivanhoe,
Which every boy has a right to know.

I had a mother who read to me tales
Of Gelert the hound of the hills of Wales,
True to his trust until his tragic death,
Faithfulness blent with his final breath.

I had a mother who read to the things
That wholesome life to the boy heart brings—
Stories that stir with an upward touch
Oh, that each mother of boys were such!

You may have tangible wealth untold;
Caskets of jewels and coffers of gold.
Richer than I you can never be—
I had a mother who read to me.

Strickland Gillilan

"A Reading Mother"

Betty Grant, about 1970

Hugs

It's wondrous what a hug can do.
A hug can cheer you when you're blue
A hug can say, "I love you so",
Or, "I hate to see you go".
A hug is "Welcome back again",
And, "Great to see you! Where've you been?".
A hug can soothe a small child's pain
And bring a rainbow after rain.
The hug, there's just no doubt about it,
We scarce could live without it!
A hug delights and warms and charms,
It must be why God gave us arms.
Hugs are great for fathers and mothers,
Sweet for sisters and sweet for brothers,
And chances are your favorite aunts
Love them more than potted plants.
Kittens crave them, puppies love them;
Heads of states are not above them.
A hug can break the language barrier
And make travel so much merrier.
No need to fret about your store of 'em.
So stretch those arms without delay
And give someone a hug today.

Unknown

"A hug can say, 'I love you so'"

Janey and Johnny Grant, 1948

Where Did You Come From

Where did you come from, Baby dear?
  Out of the everywhere into here.

Where did you get those eyes so blue?
  Out of the sky as I come through.

What makes the light in them sparkle and spin?
  Some of the starry spikes left in.

Where did you get that little tear?
  I found it waiting when I got here.

What makes your forehead so smooth and high?
  A soft hand stroked it as I went by.

What makes your cheek like a warm white rose?
  I saw something better than anyone knows.

Whence that three-corner'd smile of bliss?
  Three angels gave me at once a kiss.

Where did you get that pearly ear?
  God spoke, and it came out to hear.

Where did you get those arms and hands?
  Love made itself into hooks and bands.

Feet, whence did you come, you darling things?
  From the same box in the cherubs wings.

How did they all come just to be you?
God thought of me, and so I grew.

But how did you come to us, you dear?
God thought of you, and so I am here.

George MacDonald

"God thought of you, and so I am here"

Betty with granddaughter Samantha Schultz, 1989

Samantha's Poems

People

People need
to feel their
sadness
before the pass
of time
and breathe all
the feelings out.
Nature
helps you
like water
helps the
flowers.
And you
help Nature
and all the
people too.
And all the
world you help.

Mother Nature

Trees are nice
Because Mother Nature
Makes Them.
Mother Nature
Is a part
Of us.
We are a part of
Mother Nature.
Mother Nature
And God are
Friends.
Be Nice
To Mother Nature.

The Sky Is Pink

To me the sky is pink
and the flowers are green
and the grass is purple
and the moon is a very nice place.

And the sun is a glittering princess
and China is a magical place
where doves fly free.

And nobody knows but me.
Nobody knows but me.

I Have A Different Shadow

I have a different shadow
than the other one
It hates the light and likes the dark.

And what do you think about that?
Yes, what do you think about that?

Flying Love

Of course love is pretty,
And of course love is witty.
But love goes a-flying
in the sky.

I love love but
have to say goodbye
Cause love goes a-flying
in the sky.

Love is nice
But sometimes turns to ice.
And love goes a-flying
in the sky.

I like love
and love likes me
And love goes a-flying
in the sky.

Samantha Schultz

"And nobody knows but me"

Samantha on her first day of Nursery School, 1990

Attachment

Not flesh of my flesh,
Nor bone of my bone,
But still miraculously my own,
Never forget for a minute
That you didn't grow under my heart—but in it.

Fleur Conkling Heyliger

Little Things

Little drops of water,
Little grains of sand,
Make the mighty ocean
And the pleasant land.

Thus the little minutes
Humble though they may be,
Make the mighty ages
Of eternity.

Julia A. Fletcher

Give me a good digestion, Lord
and something to digest;
Give me a healthy body, Lord,
with sense to keep it at its best;
Give me a healthy mind, good Lord,
to keep the pure and good in sight;
Which, seeing sin is not appalled,
but finds the way to set it right.

Give me a mind that is not bored;
that doesn't whimper, whine or sigh;
Don't let me worry over much
about the fussy thing called I,
Give me a sense of humor, Lord;
give me the grace to see a joke,
To get some happiness from life
and pass it one to other folk.

Unknown

My Influence

My life shall touch a dozen lives
before this day is done,
Leave countless marks for good or ill
ere sets the evening sun.
This is the wish I always wish,
the prayer I always pray:
"Lord, may my life help other lives
it touches by the way."

Unknown

Commit thy works unto the Lord,
and thy thoughts shall be established.
—*Proverbs 16:3*

So teach us to number our days,
that we may apply our hearts unto wisdom.
—*Psalm 90:12*

Go thy way; as thou hast believed,
so it be done unto thee.
—*Matthew 8:13*

The Bible

The Children's Hour

Between the dark and the daylight,
When night is beginning to lower,
Comes a pause in the day's occupations
That is known as the Children's Hour.

I hear in the Chamber above me
The patter of little feet,
The sound of a door that is opened,
And voices soft and sweet.

From my study I see in the lamplight,
Descending the broad hall stair,
Grave Alice, and laughing Allegra,
And Edith with the golden hair.

A whisper, and then a silence:
Yet I know by their merry eyes
They are plotting and planning together
To take me by surprise.

A sudden rush from the stairway,
A sudden raid from the hall!
By the doors left unguarded,
They enter my castle wall!

They climb up into my turret
O'er the arms and back of my chair;
If I try to escape, they surround me,
They seem to be everywhere.

They almost devour me with kisses,
Their arms about me entwine,
Till I think of the Bishop of Bingen
In his mouse tower on the Rhine!

Do you think, O blue-eyed banditti,
Because you have scaled the wall,
Such an old mustache as I am
Is not a match for you all?

I have you fast in my fortress,
And will not let you depart,
But put you down into the dungeon
In the round-tower of my heart.

And there I will keep you forever,
Yes, forever and a day,
Till the wall shall crumble to ruin
And molder in dust away!

Henry Wadsworth Longfellow

"In the round tower of my heart"

*Betty's children: Johnny (top row), Janey (middle)
and Laura (bottom row). Also Betty with the two eldest
"banditti", Johnny and Janey, 1948.*

The Swing

How do you like to go up in a swing,
Up in the air so blue?
Oh, I do think it's the pleasantest thing
Ever a child can do!

Up in the air and over the wall,
Till I can see so wide,
Rivers and trees and cattle and all
Over the countryside—

Till I look down on the garden green,
Down on the roof so brown—
Up in the air I go flying again,
Up in the air and down!

Robert Lewis Stevenson

Formula for youth—
Keep your enthusiasms and forget your birthdays.

Growing old is only a bad habit
which a busy person has no time to form.

There is nothing wrong with the younger generation
that twenty years won't cure.

May you live all the days of your life.

Selected Sayings

Those attributes which keep the mind young can be wrapped up in one word: Commitment. Commitment implies interest, a willingness to take risks. The firmer one's commitment, the less likely one is to be drained or beaten by life. The occasional tendency of an unmarried woman to age faster than a married woman has less to do with any condition intrinsic to marriage than with the fact that there may well have been in the single woman's attitude something that kept her from committing herself to live in the first place.

Dr Hollis E. Clow

Hiawatha's Childhood

By the shores of Gitche Gumee,
By the shining Big-Sea-Water,
Stood the wigwam of Nokomis,
Daughter of the Moon, Nokomis.
Dark behind it rose the forest,
Rose the black and gloomy pine-trees,
Rose the firs with cones upon them;
Bright before it beat the water,
Beat the clear and sunny water,
Beat the shining Big-Sea-Water.
There the wrinkled old Nokomis
Nursed the little Hiawatha,
Rocked him in his linden cradle,
Bedded soft in moss and rushes,
Safely bound with reindeer sinews;
Stilled his fretful wail by saying,
"Hush! the Naked Bear will hear thee!"
Lulled him into slumber, singing,
"Ewa-yea! my little owlet!
Who is this, that lights the wigwam?
With his great eyes lights the wigwam?
Ewa-yea! my little owlet!"
Many things Nokomis taught him
Of the stars that shine in heaven;
Showed him Ishkoodah, the comet,
Ishkoodah, with fiery tresses;
Showed the Death-Dance of the spirits,
Warriors with their plumes and war-clubs,
Flaring far away to northward
In the frosty nights of Winter;

Showed the broad white road in heaven,
Pathway of the ghosts, the shadows,
Running straight across the heavens,
Crowded with the ghosts, the shadows.
At the door on summer evenings
Sat the little Hiawatha;
Heard the whispering of the pine-trees,
Heard the lapping of the water,
Sounds of music, words of wonder;
"Minne-wawa!" said the Pine-trees,
"Mudway-aushka!" said the water.
Saw the fire-fly, Wah-wah-taysee,
Flitting through the dusk of evening,
With the twinkle of its candle
Lighting up the brakes and bushes,
And he sang the song of children,
Sang the song Nokomis taught him:
"Wah-wah-taysee, little fire-fly,
Little, flitting, white-fire insect,
Little, dancing, white-fire creature,
Light me with your little candle,
Ere upon my bed I lay me,
Ere in sleep I close my eyelids!"
Saw the moon rise from the water
Rippling, rounding from the water,
Saw the flecks and shadows on it,
Whispered, "What is that, Nokomis?"
And the good Nokomis answered:
"Once a warrior, very angry,
Seized his grandmother, and threw her
Up into the sky at midnight;
Right against the moon he threw her;
'Tis her body that you see there."
Saw the rainbow in the heaven,
In the eastern sky, the rainbow,
Whispered, "What is that, Nokomis?"
And the good Nokomis answered:
"'Tis the heaven of flowers you see there;

All the wild-flowers of the forest,
All the lilies of the prairie,
When on earth they fade and perish,
Blossom in that heaven above us."
When he heard the owls at midnight,
Hooting, laughing in the forest,
"What is that?" he cried in terror,
"What is that," he said, "Nokomis?"
And the good Nokomis answered:
"That is but the owl and owlet,
Talking in their native language,
Talking, scolding at each other."
Then the little Hiawatha
Learned of every bird its language,
Learned their names and all their secrets,
How they built their nests in Summer,
Where they hid themselves in Winter,
Talked with them whene'er he met them,
Called them "Hiawatha's Chickens."
Of all beasts he learned the language,
Learned their names and all their secrets,
How the beavers built their lodges,
Where the squirrels hid their acorns,
How the reindeer ran so swiftly,
Why the rabbit was so timid,
Talked with them whene'er he met them,
Called them "Hiawatha's Brothers."

Henry Wadsworth Longfellow
(From *The Song of Hiawatha*)

My Shadow

I have a little shadow that goes in and out with me,
And what can be the use of him is more than I can see.
He is very, very like me from heels up to the head;
And I see him jump before me, when I jump into my bed.

The funniest thing about him is the way he likes to grow—
Not at all like the proper children, which is always very slow;
For he sometimes shoots up taller like an India-rubber ball,
And sometimes he gets so little there's none of him at all.

He hasn't got a notion of how children ought to play,
And can only make a fool of me in every sort of way.
He stays so close beside me, he's a coward you can see;
I'd think shame to stick to nursie as that shadow sticks to me!

One morning, very early, before the sun was up,
I rose and found the shining dew on every buttercup;
But my lazy little shadow, like an arrant sleepyhead,
Had stayed at home behind me and was fast asleep in bed.

Robert Lewis Stevenson

The Bear Story

That Alex "ist maked up his-own-se'f"

W'y, wunst they wuz a Little Boy went out
In the woods to shoot a Bear, So, he went out
'Way in the grea'-big woods—he did—An' he
Wuz goin' along—an' goin' along, you know,
An' purty soon he heerd somepin' go "Wooh!"
Ist thataway—"Woo-ooh!" An' he wuz skeered,
He wuz. An' so he runned an' clumbed a tree—
A grea'-big tree, he did—A sickamore—tree.
An' nen he heerd it, ag'in: an' he looked round,
An' 't'us a Bear—real-big shore-'nuff Bear!—
No: 't'uz two Bears, it wuz—two grea'-big Bears—
One of 'em wuz—ist one's a grea'-big Bear.—
But they ist boff went "Wooh!"—An' here they come
To climb the tree an' git the Little Boy
An' eat him up! An' the Little Boy
He wuz skeered worse'n ever! An' here come
The grea' big Bear a-climbin' th' tree to git
The Little Boy an' eat him up—Oh, no!—
It 'uzn't the Big Bear 'at clumb the tree—
It 'uz the Little Bear. So here he come
Climbin' the tree—an' climbin' the tree! Nen when
He git wite clost't to the Little Boy, w'y nen
The Little Boy he ist pulled up his gun
An' shot the Bear, he did, an' killed him dead!
An' nen the Bear he falled clean on down out
The tree—away clean to the ground he did—
Spling-splung! he falled plum down, and killed him, too!
An' lit wite side o' where the Big Bear's at.

———

60

An' the Big Bear's awful mad, you bet!—
'Cause—'cause the Little boy he shot his gun
An' killed the Little Bear.—'Cause the Big Bear
He—he 'uz the Little Bear's Papa.—An' so here
He come to climb the big old tree an' git
The Little Boy an' eat him up! An' when
The Little Boy he saw the grea'-big Bear
A-comin', he 'uz badder skeered, he wuz,
Than any time! An' so he think he'll climb
Up higher—'way up higher in the tree
Than the old Bear kin climb, you know.—But he—
He can't climb higher 'an old Bears kin climb,—
'Cause Bears kin climb up higher in the trees
Than any little Boys in all the Wo-r-r-ld!
An' here come the grea'-big Bear, he did,—
A'climbin' up—an' up the tree, to git
The Little boy an' eat him up! An' so
The Little boy he clumbed on higher, an' higher—
An' higher up the tree—an' higher—an' higher—
An' higher'n iss-here house is!—An' here come
The old Bear—clos'ter to him all the time!—
An' nen—first thing you know,—when th' old Big Bear
Wuz wite clos't to him—nen the Little Boy
Ist jabbed his gun wite in the old Bear's mouf
An' shot and killed him dead!—No; I forgot,—
He didn't shoot the grea'-big Bear at all—
'Cause they 'uz no load in the gun, you know—
'Cause when he shot the Little Bear, w'y, nen
No load 'uz any more nen in the gun!
But the Little Boy clumbed higher up, he did—
He clumbed lots higher—an' on up higher—an' higher
An' higher—tel he ist can't climb no higher,
'Cause nen the limbs 'uz all so little, 'way
Up in the teeny-weeny tip-top of
The tree, they'd break down wiv him ef he don't
Be keerful! So he stop an' think: An' nen
He look around—An' here come the old Bear!
An' so the Little Boy make up his mind

—

He's got to ist git out o' there some-way!—
'Cause here come the old Bear!—so clos't, his bref's
Purt' nigh so's he kin feel how hot it is
Ag'inst his bare feet—ist like old 'Ring's' bref
When he's be'n out a-huntin' an' 'a all tired.
So when th' old Bear's so clos't—the Little Boy
Ist gives a grea'-big jump fer 'nother tree—
No!—no he don't do that!—I tell you what
The Little Boy does:—W'y, nen—w'y he—Oh, yes!—
The Little Boy he finds a hole up there
'At's in the tree—an' climbs in there an' hides—
An' nen th' old Bear can't find the Little Boy
At all!—but purty soon the old Bear finds
The Little Boy's gun 'at's up there—'cause the gun
It's too tall to tooked wiv him in the hole.
So, when the old Bear find' the gun, he knows
The Little Boy's ist hid around somers there,—
An' th' old Bear 'gins to snuff and sniff around,
An' sniff an' snuff around—so's he kin find
Out where the Little Boy's hid at.—An' nen—nen—
Oh, yes!—W'y purty soon the old Bear climbs
'Way out on a big limb—a grea'-long limb,—
An' nen the Little boy climbs out the hole
An' takes his ax an' chops the limb off . . . Nen
The old Bear falls k-splunge! clean to the ground,
An' bu'st an' kill hiss'f plum dead, he did!
An' nen the Little Boy he git his gun
An' 'menced a-climbin' down the tree ag'in—
No!—no, he didn't git his gun—'cause when
The Bear falled, nen the gun falled, too—An' broked
It all to pieces, too—An' nicest gun!—
His Pa ist buyed it!—An' the Little Boy
Ist cried, he did, an' went on climbin' down
The tree—an' climbin' down—an' climbin' down!—
An' sir! when he uz purt nigh down,—W'y, nen
The old Bear he jumped up ag'in!—an' he
Ain't dead at all—ist 'tendin' thata-way,
So he can get the Little Boy an' eat

Him up! But the Little Boy he uz too smart
To climb clean down the tree.—An' the old Bear
He can't climb up the tree no more—'cause when
He fell, he broke one of his—He broke all
His legs—an' nen he couldn't climb! But he
Ist won't go 'way an' let the Little boy
Come down out of the tree. An' the old Bear
Ist growled round there, he does—ist growls an' goes
"Wooh!—Woo-ooh!" all the time! An' Little Boy
He haf to stay up in the tree—all night—
An' 'thout no supper neever—Only they
Wuz apples on the tree!—An' Little Boy
Et apples—ist all night—an' cried—an' cried!
Nen when 't'uz morning the old Bear went "Wooh!"
Ag'in, an' try to climb up the tree
An' git the Little Boy—But he can't
Climb t' save his soul, he can't!—An' oh he's mad!—
He ist tear up the ground! an' go "Woo-ooh!"
An'—Oh, yes!—purty soon, when morning's come
All light—so's you kin see, you know, w'y, nen
The old Bear finds the Little boy's gun, you know,
'At's on the ground—(An' it ain't broke at all—
I ist said that!) An' so the old Bear think
He'll take the gun an' shoot the Little Boy:—
But Bears they don't know much 'bout shootin' guns:
So when he go to shoot the Little Boy
The old Bear got the other end the gun
Ag'in his shoulder, 'sted o' th' other end—
So when he try to shoot the Little Boy,
It shot the Bear, it did—an' killed him dead!
An' nen the Little Boy clumb down the tree
An' chopped his old woolly head off,—Yes and killed
The other Bear ag'in, he did—an' killed
All boff the bears, he did—an' tuk 'em home
An' cooked 'em, too, an' et 'em!
        —An' that's all.

James Whitcomb Riley

63

The Rainbow

My heart leaps up when I behold
A rainbow in the sky:
So it was when my life began;
So it is now I am a Man;
So be it when I grow old,
Or let me die!
The Child is Father of the Man;
And I could wish my days to be
Bound each to each with natural piety.

William Wordsworth

Griggsby's Station

Pap's got his patent-right, and rich as all creation;
But where's the peace and comfort that we all had before?
Le's go a-visitin' back to Griggsby's Station—
Back to where we ust to be so happy and so pore!

The likes of us a-livin' here! It's jes' a mortal pity
To see us in this great big house with carpets on the stairs,
And the pump right in the kitchen! And the city! city! city!—
And nothin' but the city all around us ever-where's!

Climb clean above the roof and look from the steeple,
And never see a robin, nor a beech or ellum tree!
And right here in ear-shot of at least a thousan' people,
And none that neighbors with us or we want to go and see!

Let's go a-visitin back to Griggsby's Station—
Back where the latch-string's a-hangin' from the door,
And ever' neighbor round the place is dear as a relation—
Back to where we ust to be so happy and so pore!

I want to see the Wiggenses, the whole kit-and bilin',
And drive up from Shallow Ford to stay the Sunday through;
And I want to see 'em hitchin' at their son-in-law's and pilin'
Out there at 'Lizy Ellen's like they ust to do!

I want to see the piece-quilts the Jones girls is makin';
And I want to pester Laury 'bout their freckled hired hand,
And joke her 'bout the widower she come purt nigh a-takin',
Till her Pap got his pension 'lowed in time to save his land.

Let's go a-visitin' back to Griggsby's Station—
Back to where there's nothing aggervatin' any more,
Shet away safe in the woods around the old location—
Back to where we ust to be so happy and so pore.

I want to see Marindy and help her with her sewin',
And hear her talk so lovin' of her man that's dead and gone,
And stand up with Emanuel to show me how he's growin'
And smile as I have saw her 'fore she put her mournin' on.

I want to see the Samples, on the old lower eighty,
Where John our oldest boy, he was tuk and burried—for
His own sake and Katy's—and I want to cry with Katy
As she reads all his letters over, writ from The War.

What's in all this grand life and high situation,
And nary pink nor hollyhawk a-bloomin' at the door?—
Le's go a-visitin' back to Griggsby's Station—
Back where we ust to be so happy and so pore!

James Whitcomb Riley

"Back where we ust to be so happy and so pore"

Haynes Homestead, belonging to the family of Fred's mother,
Florence McPherson Haynes Grant,
in western Oklahoma, about 1900

The Raggedy Man

O the Raggedy Man! He works fer Pa;
An' he's the goodest man ever you saw!
He comes to our house every day,
An' waters the horses an' feeds 'em hay;
An' he opens the shed—an' we all ist laugh
When he drives out our little old wobble-ly calf;
An' nen—ef our hired girl says he can—
He milks the cow for 'Lizabuth Ann—
Ain't he a' awful good Raggedy Man?
Raggedy! Raggedy! Raggedy Man!

Why, The Raggedy Man—he's ist so good,
He splits the kindlin' an' chops the wood;
An' nen he spades in our garden, too,
An' does most things 'at boys can't do.—
He climbed clean up in our big tree
An' shooked a' apple down for me—
An' 'nother'n', too, for 'Lizabuth Ann—
An' 'nother'n', too, fer The Raggedy Man—
Ain't he a' awful kind Raggedy Man?
Raggedy! Raggedy! Raggedy Man!

An' The Raggedy Man one time say he
Pick' roast' rambos from a' orchurd tree,
An' et 'em—all ist roast' an' hot!—
An' it's so, too!—'cause a corn-crib got
Afire one time an' all burn down

On 'The Smoot Farm,' 'bout four mile from town—
On 'The Smoot Farm'! Yes—an' the hired han'
'At worked there nen 'uz The Raggedy Man!—
Ain't he the beatin'est Raggedy Man?
Raggedy! Raggedy! Raggedy Man!

The Raggedy Man's so good an' kind
He'll be our 'horsey,' an' 'haw' an' mind
Ever'thing 'at you make him do—
An' won't run off—'less you want him to!
I drived him wunst way down our lane
An' he got skeered, when it 'menced to rain,
An' ist rared up an' squealed and run
Purt' nigh away!—an' it's all in fun!
Nen he skeered ag'in at a' old tin can . . .
Whoa! y' old runaway Raggedy Man!
Raggedy! Raggedy! Raggedy Man!

An' The Raggedy Man, he knows most rhymes,
An' tells 'em, ef I be good, sometimes;
Knows 'bout giunts, an' Griffuns, an' Elves,
An' the Squidgicum-squees 'at swallers the'rselves
An', rite by the pump in our pasture-lot,
He showed me the hole 'at the Wunks is got,
At lives 'way deep in the ground, an' can
Turn into me, er 'Lizabuth Ann!
Er Ma, er Pa, er The Raggedy Man!
Ain't he a funny old Raggedy Man?
Raggedy! Raggedy! Raggedy Man!

An' wunst when The Raggedy Man come late,
An' pigs ist root' thue the garden-gate,
He 'tend like the pigs 'uz bears an' said
"Old Bear-shooter'll shoot 'em dead!"
An' race' an' chase' 'em an' they'd ist run

———

When he pint his hoe at 'em like it's a gun
An' go "Bang—Bang!" nen 'tend he stan'
An' load up his gun ag'in! Raggedy Man!
He's an old Bear-shooter Raggedy Man!
Raggedy! Raggedy! Raggedy Man!

An' sometimes The Raggedy Man lets on
We're little prince-children, an' old King's gone
To git more money, an' lef' us there—
And Robbers is ist thick ever'where;
An' nen—ef we all won't cry, fer shore—
The Raggedy Man he'll come and 'splore
The Castul-Halls, an' steal the 'gold'—
An' steal us, too, an' grab an' hold
An' pack us off to his old 'Cave'!—An'
Haymow's the 'cave' o' The Raggedy Man!—
Raggedy! Raggedy! Raggedy Man!

The Raggedy Man—one time, when he
Wuz makin' a little bow-'n'-orry fer me,
Says "When you're big like your Pa is,
Air you go' to keep a fine store like his—
An' be a rich merchunt—an' wear fine clothes?—
Er what air you go' to be, goodness knows?"
An' nen he laughs at Lizabuth Ann,
An' I says "'M go' be a nice Raggedy Man!—
I'm ist go' to be a nice Raggedy Man!"
Raggedy! Raggedy! Raggedy Man!

James Whitcomb Riley

Out To Old Aunt Mary's

Wasn't it pleasant, O brother mine,
In those old days of the lost sunshine
Of youth—when the Saturday's chores were through,
And the "Sunday's wood" in the kitchen, too,
And we went visiting, "me and you",
Out to Old Aunt Mary's?—

"Me and you"—And the morning fair,
With the dewdrops twinkling everywhere;
The scent of the cherry-blossoms blown
After us, in the roadway lone,
Our capering shadows onward thrown—

Out to Old Aunt Mary's!
It all comes back so clear to-day!
Though I am as bald as you are gray,—
Out by the barn-lot and down the lane
We patter along in the dust again,
As light as the tips of the drops of the rain,
Out to Old Aunt Mary's.

The few last houses of the town;
Then on, up the high creek-bluffs and down;
Past the squat toll-gate with its well-sweep pole,
The bridge, and 'the old-babtizin'-hole;'
Loitering, awed, o'er pool and shoal,
Out to Old Aunt Mary's.

We cross the pasture, and through the wood,
Where the old gray snag of the poplar stood,
Where the hammering 'red-heads' hopped awry,
And the buzzard raised in the clearing-sky
  And lolled and circled, as we went by
    Out to Old Aunt Mary's.

Or, stayed by the glint of the redbird's wings,
Or the glitter of song that the bluebird sings,
All hushed we feign to strike strange trails,
As the "big braves" do in the Indian tales,
  Till again our real quest lags and fails—
    Out to Old Aunt Mary's.—

And the woodland echoes with yells of mirth
That make old war-whoops of minor worth! . . . .
  Where such heroes of war as we?—
  With bows and arrows of fantasy,
  Chasing each other from tree to tree
    Out to Old Aunt Mary's!

Then in the dust of the road again;
And the teams we met, and the countrymen;
And the long highway, with sunshine spread
  As thick as butter on country bread
Our cares behind, and our hearts ahead
    Out to Old Aunt Mary's.—

For only, now, at the road's next bend
To the right we could make out the gable-end
Of the fine old Huston homestead—not
  Half a mile from the sacred spot
Where dwelt our Saint in her simple cot—
    Out to Old Aunt Mary's.

Why I see her now in the open door
Where the little gourds grew up the sides and o'er
The clapboards roof!—And her face—ah, me!
Wasn't it good for a boy to see—
And wasn't it good for a boy to be
Out to Old Aunt Mary's?—

The jelly—the jam and the marmalade,
And the cherry and quince "preserves" she made!
And the sweet-sour pickles of peach and pear,
With cinnamon in 'em, and all things rare!—
And the more we ate was the more to spare,
Out to Old Aunt Mary's!

Ah! was there, ever, so kind a face
And gentle as hers, or such a grace
Of welcoming, as she cut the cake
Or the juicy pies that she joyed to make
Just for the visiting children's sake—
Out to Old Aunt Mary's!

The honey, too, in its amber comb
One only finds in an old farm-home;
And the coffee, fragrant and sweet, and ho!
So hot that we gloried to drink it so,
With spangles of tears in our eyes, you know—
Out to Old Aunt Mary's.

And the romps we took, in our glad unrest!—
Was it the lawn that we loved the best,
With its swooping swing in the locust trees,
Or was it the grove, with its leafy breeze,
Or the dim haymow, with its fragrancies—
Out to Old Aunt Mary's

———

Far fields, bottom-lands, creek-banks—all,
We ranged at will.—Where the waterfall
Laughed all day as it slowly poured
Over the dam by the old mill-ford
While the tail-race writhed, and the mill-wheel roared—
Out to Old Aunt Mary's.

But home, with Aunty in nearer call,
That was the best place, after all—
The talks on the back porch, in the low
Slanting sun and the evening glow,
With the voice of counsel that touched us so,
Out to Old Aunt Mary's.

And then in the garden—near the side
Where the beehives were and the path was wide—
The apple-house—like a fairy cell—
With the little square door we knew so well,
And the wealth inside but our tongues could tell
Out to Old Aunt Mary's.

And the old spring-house, in the cool green gloom
Of the willow trees,—and the cooler room
Where the swinging shelves and the crocks were kept,
Where the cream in a golden langor slept,
Where the waters gurgled and laughed and wept—
Out to Old Aunt Mary's.

And many a time have you and I—
Barefoot boys in days gone by—
Knelt, and in tremulous ecstasies
Dipped our lips into sweets like these,—
Memory is now on her knees
Out to Old Aunt Mary's.—

For, O my brother so far away,
This is to tell you—she waits to-day
To welcome us:—Aunt Mary fell
Asleep this morning, whispering, "Tell
The boys to come." . . . . And all is well
Out to Old Aunt Mary's.

James Whitcomb Riley

"Such a grace of welcoming"

*Entryway to the home of Betty's son, John Grant,
and his wife Janet, in Rhode Island,
evocative of* "Old Aunt Mary's"

Little Orphant Annie

Inscribed With All Faith And Affection

To all the little children:—The happy ones; and sad ones;
The sober and the silent ones; the boisterous and glad ones;
The good ones—Yes, the good ones, too; and all the lovely bad ones.

Little Orphant Annie's come to our house to stay,
An' wash the cups and saucers up, and brush the crumbs
    away,
An' shoo the chickens off the porch, an' dust the hearth,
    an' sweep,
An' make the fire, and bake the bread, an' earn her board-
    an-keep.
An' all us childern, when the supper-things is done,
We set around the kitchen fire an' has the mostest fun,
A-listenin' to the witch tales 'at Annie tells about,
And the Gobble-uns at gits you
                Ef you
                  Don't
                    Watch
                      Out!

Wunst they wuz a little boy wouldn't say his prayers,
An' when he went to bed at night, away up-stairs,
His Mammy heerd him holler, an' his Daddy heerd him
  bawl,
An' when they turn't the kivvers down, he wuzn't there at all!
An' they seeked him in the rafter-room, an' cubby hole,
  an' press,
An' seeked him up the chimbly-flue, and ever'wheres, I
  guess;
But all they ever found wuz thist his pants an' roundabout!
An' the Gobble-uns'll git you
                    Ef you
                        Don't
                           Watch
                              Out!

An' one time a little girl 'ud allus laugh and grin,
An' make fun of ever'one, an' all her blood-and-kin;
An' wunst when they wuz "company" an' ole folks wuz there,
She mocked 'em and shocked 'em an' said she didn't care!
An' thist as she kicked her heels, an' turn't to run and hide,
They wuz two great big Black Things a-standin' by her side,
An' they snatched her through the ceilin' 'fore she
  knowed what she's about!
And the Gobble-uns'll git you
                    Ef you
                        Don't
                           Watch
                              Out!

77

And Little Orphant Annie says, when the blaze is blue,
An' the lamp-wick sputters, an' the wind goes woo-oo!
An' you hear the crickets quit, an' the moon is gray,
An' the lightnin' bugs in dew is all squenched away—
You had better mind yer parunts, an' yer teachers fond
    an' dear,
An' cherish them at loves you, an' dry the orphants tear,
An' he'p the pore and needy ones 'at clusters all about,
Er the Gobble-uns'll git you
                Ef you
                   Don't
                      Watch
                         Out!

James Whitcomb Riley

Think About The Lovely Things

Think about the lovely things
That bless our lives each day,
Little lives to cherish
That comes along the way—

The birds' sweet song, the leafy trees,
The smallest flowers that bloom,
Timid sunbeams peeking in
To brighten up a room—

For each of these remind us,
Though cares may come our way,
There's a little bit of happiness
In every passing day.

God give you strength for all your needs,
And rest and comfort too—
God bless you with His perfect love,
And grant good health to you.

Unknown

Wynken, Blynken, And Nod

Wynken, Blynken, and Nod one night
Sailed off in a wooden shoe—
Sailed on a river of crystal light,
Into a sea of dew.
"Where are you going, and what do you wish?"
The old moon asked the three.
"We have come to fish for the herring fish
That live in the beautiful sea;
Nets of silver and gold have we!"
Said Wynken,
Blynken,
And Nod.

The old moon laughed and sang a song,
As they rocked in the wooden shoe,
And the wind that sped them all night long
Ruffled the waves of dew.
The little stars were the herring fish,
That lived in that beautiful sea—
"Now cast your nets wherever you wish—
Never afeared are we;"
So cried the stars to the fishermen three:
Wynken,
Blynken,
And Nod.

All night long their nets they threw
To the stars in the twinkling foam—
Then down from the stars came the wooden shoe,
Bringing the fishermen home;
'Twas all so pretty a sail it seemed
As if it could not be,
And some folks thought 'twas a dream they'd dreamed
Of sailing that beautiful sea—
But I shall name you the fishermen three:
Wynken,
Blynken,
And Nod.

Wynken and Blynken are two little eyes,
And Nod is a little head,
And the wooden shoe that sailed the skies
Is a wee one's trundle-bed.
So shut your eyes while your mother sings
Of wonderful sights that be,
And you shall see the beautiful things
As you rock in the misty sea,
Where the old shoe rocked the fishermen three:
Wynken,
Blynken,
And Nod.

Eugene Fields

The Duel

The gingham dog and the calico cat
Side by side on the table sat;
'Twas half past twelve, and (what do you think!)
Nor one or t'other had slept a wink!
The old Dutch clock and the Chinese plate
Appeared to know as sure as fate
There was going to be a terrible spat.

(I wasn't there; I simply state
What was told me by the Chinese plate!)

The gingham dog went "bow-wow-wow!"
And the calico cat replied "mee-ow!"
The air was littered, an hour or so,
With bits of gingham and calico,
While the old Dutch clock in the chimney-place
Up with its hands before its face,
For it always dreaded a family row!

(Now mind: I'm only telling you
What the old Dutch clock declares is true!)

The Chinese plate looked very blue,
And wailed, "Oh, dear! What shall we do!"
But the gingham dog and the calico cat
Wallowed this way and tumbled that,
Employing every tooth and claw
In the awfulest way you ever saw—
And, oh, how the gingham and calico flew!

*(Don't fancy I exaggerate—I got my news
from the Chinese plate!)*

The next morning where the two had sat
They found no trace of the dog or cat;
And some folks think unto this day
That burglars stole that pair away!
But the truth about the cat and pup
Is this: they ate each other up!
Now what do you think of that!

*(The old Dutch clock it told me so,
And that is how I came to know!)*

Eugene Fields

Laura Altevers

"The gingham dog went 'bow-wow-wow!'
And the calico cat replied 'mee-ow!'"

New Friends And Old Friends

Make new friends, but keep the old,
Those are the silver, these are the gold.
New-made friendships, like new wine,
Age will mellow and refine,
Friendships that have stood the test—
Time and change—are surely best,
Brow may wrinkle, hair grow gray,
Friendship never knows decay,
For 'mid old friends, tried and true,
Once more we our youth renew,
But old friends, alas, may die,
New friends their place supply,
Cherish friendship in your breast—
New is good, but old is best,
Make new friends, but keep the old,
Those are silver, these are gold.

Joseph Parry

Do Not Find Fault

Do not find fault with the man who limps,
Or stumbles along the road,
Unless you have worn the shoes he wears,
Or struggled beneath his load.
There may be tacks in his shoes that hurt,
Though hidden away from view.
Or the burden he bears, placed upon your back,
Might cause you to stumble, too.

Don't sneer at the man who is down today,
Unless you have felt the blow
That caused his fall, or felt the same
That only the fallen know.
You may be strong, but still the blows
That were his, if dealt to you,
In the selfsame way at the selfsame time,
Might cause you to stagger, too.

Don't be harsh with the man who sins,
Or pelt him with wood or stone,
Unless you are sure, yes, doubly sure,
That you have no sins of your own.
For, you know, perhaps the tempter's voice
Should whisper soft to you,
As it did to him when he went astray,
'Twould cause you to falter, too.

Unknown

Our Own

If I had known in the morning
How wearily all the day
The words unkind would trouble my mind
That I said when you went away,
I had been more careful, darling,
Nor given you needless pain;
But we vex our own with look and tone
We may never take back again.

For though in the quiet evening
You may give me the kiss of peace,
Yet it well might be that never for me
The pain of the heart should cease!
How many go forth at morning
Who never come home at night!
And hearts have broken for harsh words spoken
That sorrow can ne'er set right.

We have careful thought for the stranger,
And smiles for the sometime guest;
But oft for "our own" the bitter tone,
Though we love our own the best.
Ah! Lips with the curve impatient.
Ah! Brow with the shade of scorn,
'Twere a cruel fate, were the night too late
To undo the work of the morn!

Margaret Sangster

A Creed For Later Years

I hope I will always appreciate new thoughts,
new ideas, and the life of the mind.

I hope I will always take time to listen
to the opinions of others.

I hope I will not stop exploring the best of everything
in a changing world.

I hope I will be called wise but not opinionated.

I hope I will be considered a person of innate
dignity and not a prude.

I hope that all I have learned along the way
will not go to waste.

I hope I will remember when I am slowing down
that it wasn't easy being young.

I hope I will like myself a lot—just as I am.

I hope my grown children and my grandchildren
will be, above all else, my best friends.

I hope I am never too old to change—my home,
my activities, my priorities, my point of view.

I hope I will never call my time limited,
but instead realize that it is its quality,
not its quantity, that counts.

I hope I can laugh—at least once every day.

Unknown

Stone walls do not a prison make,
Nor iron bars a cage;
Minds innocent and quiet take
That for a hermitage:
If I have freedom in my love
And in my soul am free,
Angels alone; that soar above,
Enjoy such liberty.

Richard Lovelace
(From *To Althea, From Prison*)

Three Gates

If you are tempted to reveal
A tale to you someone had told
About another, make it pass,
Before you speak, three gates of gold.
Three narrow gates: First, "Is it true?"
Then, "Is it needful?" In your mind
Give truthful answer. And the next
Is last and narrowest, "Is it kind?"
And if to reach your lips at last
It passes through these gateways three,
Then you may tell the tale, nor fear
What the results of speech may be.

Arabian Proverb
(A *Hadees* of the Prophet Muhammed)

Man's capacity for justice makes democracy possible.
Man's tendency for injustice makes democracy
necessary.

Rheinhold Niebuhr

Charity

There is such good in the worst of us,
And so much bad in the best of us
That it ill behooves any of us
To find fault with the rest of us.

Unknown

Say It Now

If you have a friend worth loving,
Love him. Yes, and let him know
That you love him, ere life's evening
Tinge his brow with sunset glow.
Why should good words ne'er be said
Of a friend—till he is dead?

Scatter thus your seeds of kindness
All enriching as you go—
Leave them. Trust the Harvest Giver;
He will make each seed to grow,
So till the happy end
Your life shall never lack a friend.

Unknown

The Bridge Builder

An old man, going a lone highway,
Came at the evening, cold and gray,
To a chasm, vast and deep and wide,
Through which was flowing a sullen tide.
The old man crossed in the twilight dim—
That sullen stream had no fears for him;
But he turned when he reached the other side,
And built a bridge to span the tide.

"Old man," said a fellow pilgrim near,
"You are wasting strength in building here.
Your journey will end with the ending day;
You will never again pass this way
You have crossed the chasm, deep and wide,
Why build the bridge at the eventide?"

The builder lifted his old gray head,
"Good friend, in the path I have come," he said,
"There followeth after me today
A youth whose feet must pass this way.
This chasm that has been naught to me
To that fair-haired youth may a pitfall be.
He, too, must cross in the twilight dim;
Good friend, I am building the bridge for him."

William Allan Dromgoole

At The Place Of The Sea

Have you come to the Red Sea place in your life,
Where, in spite of all you can do,
There is no way out, there is no way back,
There is no way but through?
Then wait on the Lord, with trust serene,
Till the night of your fear is gone;
He will send the winds, He will heap the floods,
When he says to your soul, "Go on!"
(Based on Exodus 14)

Annie Johnson Flint

―

I Said A Prayer For You Today

I said a prayer for you today
And know God must have heard—
I felt the answer in my heart
Although He spoke not a word!
I didn't ask for wealth or fame
(I knew you wouldn't mind)—
I asked Him to send treasures
Of a far more lasting kind!
I asked that He be near you
At the start of each new day
To grant you health and blessings
And friends to share your way!
I asked for happiness for you
In all things great and small—
But it was for His loving care
I prayed the most of all!

Unknown

My flesh and heart faileth;
but God is the strength
of my heart and my portion forever.
—*Psalm 73:26*

Rejoicing in hope;
patient in tribulation;
continuing instant in prayer.
—*Romans 12:12*

Casting all your care upon him;
for he careth for you.
—*1 Peter 5:7*

For I am thy God,
I will strengthen thee,
yea I will help thee.
—*Isaiah 41:10*

The Bible

You Encouraged Me

I will not pass this way but once.
Too soon life's journey ends.
Then may I be a friend to others,
As you have been my friend.

As you've encouraged me with praise
When I became discouraged,
So I'll cheer my downhearted friends
And send them forth encouraged.

I will not pass this way again
So let me rise to be
A friend to those who can't repay,
As you have been to me.

Peter Tanksley

Poems

The unrelenting thorns of pain,
And poverty's harassing cry,
That wound anew the hearts of men,
All these will die!

The ever clutching hands of greed,
And wars implacable array,
Will pack their arrows of despair,
And pass away!

For never yet was Calvary borne
Without its gift of Eastertide;
For love and faith, and sacrifice—
All these abide.

Unknown

Touch Hands

Ah friends, dear friends, as years go
On and heads get gray,
How fasts the guests do go.

Touch hands, touch hands, with those who stay.
Strong hands to weak, old hands to young,
Around the Christmas board, touch hands.

The false forget, the foe forgive,
For every guest will go and every fire burn low
And every cabin empty stand.

Forget, forgive, for who may say
That Christmas day may ever
Come to host or guest again.
Touch hands!

William Henry Harrison Murray

One immediate fruit of patience is peace:
A sweet tranquility of mind; a serenity of spirit,
which can never be found, unless where patience reigns.
And this peace often rises into joy.
Even in the midst of various temptations,
those that are enabled
'in patience to possess their soul'
can witness, not only quietness of spirit,
but triumph and exultation.

John Wesley
(From *Sermon 83*)

She Dwelt Among
The Untrodden Ways

She dwelt among untrodden ways
Besides the springs of Dove,
Maid whom there were none to praise
And very few to love.

A violet by a mossy stone
Half hidden from the eye!
—Fair as a star, when only one
Is shining in the sky.

She lived unknown, and few could know
When Lucy ceased to be;
But she is in her grave, and, oh
The difference to me.

William Wordsworth

Sweet Peril

Alas, how easily things go wrong!
A sigh too much, a kiss too long,
And there follows a mist and weeping rain,
And life is never the same again.

Alas, how hardly things go right!
'Tis hard to watch in the summer night,
For the sigh will come, and the kiss will stay,
And the summer night is a winter day.

And yet how easily things to right,
If the sigh and a kiss of a summer's night
Come deep from the soul in the stronger ray
That is born in the light of a winter's day.

And things can never go badly wrong
If the heart be true and the love be strong.
For the mist, if it comes, or the weeping rain
Will be changed by the love into sunshine again.

George MacDonald

Oh Let My Love

Like the sunlight, let my love surround you—
Refresh you like the soft sweet summer rain.
Nor ever let it be said that my love bound you,
Or hurt your heart, or caused you pain.

Oh, let my love be like a rose, fresh broken
From fragrant bough, its petals still uncrushed.
And like a trembling word that lies unspoken
Upon the lips, let my love be hushed.

Oh, let my love be beautiful and glowing,
And soft as silver moonlight on the sea.
Oh, let my love be light as light winds blowing,
For so my love will bind you fast to me.

Eva Bryon

All Paths Lead To You

All paths lead to you
Where e'er I stray,
You are the evening star
At the end of day.

All paths lead to you
Hill-top or low,
You are the white birch
In the sun's flow.

All paths lead to you
Where e'er I roam,
You are the lark-song,
Calling me home.

Blanche Shoemaker Wagstaff

"All paths lead to you"

Betty and Fred Grant on their wedding day
November 27, 1943; Richmond, Indiana

There Are Such Things

A heart that's true, there are such things,
A dream for two, there are such things,
Someone to whisper, 'Darling, you're my guiding star,
Not caring what you own, but just what you are.'

So have a little faith in what tomorrow brings,
You'll reach a star, because there are such things.

S. Adams, A. Baer, and G. W. Meyer
(Excerpt from a World War II Song)

I just kissed your picture good-night,
And now, dear, I'll turn down the light.
Your picture 'neath my pillow
Works like a charm it seems,
For you steal through my pillow into my dreams.
You know we are not really apart
For we're still in each others' heart.

Mack David and Walter Kent
(Excerpt from a World War II Song)

—

Only We

Dream no more that grief and pain
Could such hearts as ours enchain,
Safe from loss and safe from gain,
    Free, as Love makes free.

When false friends pass coldly by,
    Sigh, in earnest pity, sigh,
Turning thy unclouded eye,
    Up from them to me.

Hear not danger's trampling feet,
    Feel not sorrow's wintry sleet,
Trust that life is just and meet,
    With mine arm round thee.

Lip on lip, and eye to eye,
Love to love, we live, we die;
No more Thou, no more I,
    We, and only we!

Richard Monckton Milnes,
Lord Houghton

"Eye to eye, love to love"

Fred and Betty Grant
Dayton, Ohio 1944

A Woman's Question

Do you know you have asked for the costliest thing
    Ever made by the Hand above?
A woman's heart, and a woman's life—
    And a woman's wonderful love.

Do you know you have asked for this priceless thing
    As a child might ask for a toy?
Demanding what others have died to win,
    With the reckless dash of a boy.

You have written my lesson of duty out,
    Manlike, you have questioned me,
Now stand at the bar of my woman's soul
    Until I question thee.

You require your mutton shall always be hot,
    Your socks and your shirts be whole;
I require your heart to be true as God's stars
    And as pure as His heaven your soul.

You require a cook for your mutton and beef,
    I require a far greater thing
A seamstress you're wanting for socks and shirts—
    I look for a man and a king.

A king for the beautiful realm called Home,
    And a man that the Maker, God,
Shall look upon as He did the first
    And say, "It is very good."

I am fair and young, but the rose will fade
From my soft young cheek one day;
Will you love me then 'mid the falling leaves
As you did 'mong the blossoms of May?

Is your heart an ocean so strong and deep,
I may launch my all on the tide?
A loving woman finds heaven or hell
On the day she is made a bride.

I require all that are grand and true,
All things that a man should be;
If you give this all, I would stake my life
To be all you demand of me.

If you cannot do this, a laundress and cook
You can buy and little to pay;
But a woman's heart and a woman's life
Are not to be won that way.

Mary Torrans Lathrap

But don't be afraid that distance
and time will finally tear us apart,
The farther you go, the longer you stay,
the deeper you grow in my heart.

Betty Robinson Grant
(In a letter written to Fred during World War II)

———

The Heart Of A Girl Is A Wonderful Thing

What is the heart of a girl?
Is it something that's given to swing?
Oh! Be it whatever it may,
The heart of a girl is a wonderful thing.

What a precious gift man can obtain,
And it's something that to him brings
Love, joy and perhaps fame—
'Tis the heart of a girl, a wonderful thing.

If you be a gambler, or maybe a cheat,
When a girl comes along, ah then,
If she gives you her heart, you'll fall at her feet,
For the heart of a girl is a wonderful thing.

A heart that's wonderful and true,
A heart that's ready to sing
Except that heart there's nothing for you,
For the heart of a girl is a wonderful thing.

If you want to be happy and gay,
Listen to me, my friend,
Get the heart of a girl of today,
For it is a wonderful thing.

It will wipe away all sadness,
It will wipe away all pain;
It will bring you joy and gladness,
For the heart of a girl is a wonderful thing.

Unknown

"The heart of a girl is a wonderful thing"

Betty at Indian Lake, Logan County, Ohio; 1943

Maud Muller

Maud Muller on a summer day
Raked the meadow sweet with hay.

Beneath her torn hat glowed the wealth
Of simple beauty and rustic health.

Singing, she wrought, and her merry glee
The mock-bird echoed from his tree.

But when she glanced to the far-off town,
White from its hill-slope looking down,

The sweet song died, and a vague unrest
And a nameless longing filled her breast,—

A wish that she hardly dared to own,
For something better than she had known.

The Judge rode slowly down the lane,
Smoothing his horse's chestnut mane.

He drew his bridle in the shade
Of the apple-trees, to greet the maid,

And asked a draught from the spring that flowed
Through the meadow across the road.

She stooped where the cool spring bubbled up,
And filled for him her small tin cup,

And blushed as she gave it, looking down
On her feet so bare, and her tattered gown.

"Thanks!" said the Judge; "a sweeter draught
From a fairer hand was never quaffed."

He spoke of the grass and flowers and trees,
Of the singing birds and the humming bees.

Then talked of the haying, and wondered whether
The cloud in the west would bring foul weather.

And Maud forgot her brier-torn gown,
And her graceful ankles bare and brown;

And listened, while a pleased surprise
Looked from her long-lashed hazel eyes.

At last, like one who for delay
Seeks a vain excuse, he rode away.

Maud Muller looked and sighed; "Ah me!
That I the Judge's bride might be!

"He would dress me up in silks so fine,
And praise and toast me at his wine.

"My father should wear a broadcloth coat;
My brother should sail a painted boat.

"I'd dress my mother so grand and gay,
And the baby should have a new toy each day.

"And I'd feed the hungry and clothe the poor,
And all should bless me who left our door."

The Judge looked back as he climbed the hill
And saw Maud Muller standing still.

"A form more fair, a face more sweet,
Ne'er hath it been my lot to meet.

"And her modest answer and graceful air
Show her wise and good as she is fair.

"Would she were mine, and I today,
Like her, a harvester of hay;

"No doubtful balance of rights and wrongs,
No weary lawyers with endless tongues,

"But low of cattle and song of birds,
And health and quiet and loving words."

But he thought of his sisters, proud and cold,
And his mother, vain of her rank and gold.

So closing his heart, the Judge rode on.
And Maud was left in the field alone.

But the lawyers smiled that afternoon,
When he hummed in court an old love-tune;

And the young girl mused beside the well
Till the rain on the unraked clover fell.

He wedded a wife of richest dower,
Who lived for fashion, as he for power.

Yet oft, on his marble hearth's bright glow,
He watched a picture come and go.

And sweet Maud Muller's hazel eyes
Looked out in their innocent surprise.

Oft, when the wine in his glass was red,
He longed for the wayside well instead;

And closed his eyes on his garnished rooms
To dream of meadows and clover-blooms.

And the proud man sighed, with a secret pain,
"Ah, that I were free again"

"Free as when I rode that day,
Where the barefoot maiden raked her hay."

She wedded a man unlearned and poor,
And many children played round her door.

But care and sorrow, and childbirth pain,
Left their traces on heart and brain.

And oft, when the summer sun shone hot
On the new-mown hay in the meadow lot,

And she heard the little spring brook fall
Over the roadside, through the wall,

In the shade of the apple-tree again
She saw a rider draw his rein;

And, gazing down with timid grace,
She felt his pleased eyes read her face.

Sometimes her narrow kitchen walls
Stretched away into stately halls;

—

The weary wheel to a spinet turned,
The tallow candle an astral burned,

And for him who sat by the chimney lug,
Dozing and grumbling o'er pipe and mug,

A manly form at her side she saw,
And joy was duty and love was law.

Then she took up her burden of life again,
Saying only, "It might have been."

Alas for maiden, alas for Judge,
For rich repiner and household drudge!

God pity them both! and pity us all,
Who vainly the dreams of youth recall.

For of all sad words of tongue or pen,
The saddest are these; "It might have been."

Ah, well! for us all some sweet hope lies
Deeply buried from human eyes;

And, in the hereafter, angels may
Roll the stone from its grave away!

John Greenleaf Whittier

The Courtin'

God makes sech nights, all white an' still
Fur 'z you can look or listen,
Moonshine an' snow on field an' hill,
All silence an' all glisten.

Zekle crep' up quite unbeknown
An' peeked in thru' the winder,
An' there sot Huldy all alone,
'ith no one nigh to hinder.

A fireplace filled the room's one side
With half a cord o' wood in—
There warn't no stoves (tell comfort died)
To bake ye to a puddin'.

The wa'nut logs shot sparkles out
Towards the pootiest, bless her,
An' leetle flames danced all about
The chiny on the dresser.

Agin the chimbley crook-necks hung,
An' in amongst 'em rusted
The ole queen's-arm thet gran'ther Young
Fetched back f'om Concord busted.

The very room, coz she was in,
Seemed warm f'om floor to ceilin',
An' she looked full ez rosy agin
Ez the apples she was peelin'.

'T was kin' o' kingdom-come to look
On sech a blessed cretur,
A dogrose blushin' to a brook
Ain't modester nor sweeter.

He was six foot o' man, A 1,
Clear grit an' human natur';
None could n't quicker pitch a ton
Nor dror a furrer straighter.

He 'd sparked it with full twenty gals,
He 'd squired 'em, danced 'em, druv 'em,
Fust this one, an' then thet, by spells—
All is, he could n't love 'em.

But long o' her his veins 'ould run
All crinkly like curled maple,
The side she breshed felt full o' sun
Ez a south slope in Ap'il.

———

118

She thought no v'ice hed sech a swing
  Ez hisn in the choir;
My! when he made Ole Hunderd ring,
  She knowed the Lord was nigher.

An' she 'd blush scarlit, right in prayer,
  When her new meetin'-bunnet
Felt somehow thru' its crown a pair
  O' blue eyes sot upun it.

Thet night, I tell ye, she looked some!
  She seemed to 've gut a new soul,
For she felt sartin-sure he 'd come,
  Down to her very shoe-sole.

She heered a foot, an' knowed it tu,
  A-raspin' on the scraper,—
All ways to once her feelin's flew
  Like sparks in burnt-up paper.

He kin' o' l'itered on the mat,
  Some doubtfle o' the sekle,
His heart kep' goin' pity-pat,
  But hern went pity Zekle.

An' yit she gin her cheer a jerk
  Ez though she wished him furder,
An' on her apples kep' to work,
  Parin' away like murder.

"You want to see my Pa, I s'pose?"
"Wal .... no .... I come dasignin'"—
"To see my Ma? She 's sprinklin' clo'es
  Agin to-morrer's i'nin'."

———

119

To say why gals acts so or so,
Or don't, 'ould be presumin';
Mebby to mean yes an' say no
Comes nateral to women.

He stood a spell on one foot fust,
Then stood a spell on t' other,
An' on which one he felt the wust
He could n't ha' told ye nuther.

Says he, "I 'd better call agin";
Says she, "Think likely, Mister":
Thet last word pricked him like a pin,
An' . . . . Wal, he up an' kist her.

When Ma bimeby upon 'em slips,
Huldy sot pale ez ashes,
All kin' o' smily roun' the lips
An' teary roun' the lashes.

For she was jes' the quiet kind
Whose naturs never vary,
Like streams that keep a summer mind
Snowhid in Jenooary.

The blood clost roun' her heart felt glued
Too tight for all expressin',
Tell mother see how metters stood,
An' gin 'em both her blessin'.

Then her red come back like the tide
Down to the Bay o' Fundy,
An' all I know is they was cried
In meetin' come nex' Sunday.

James Russell Lowell

Ten Commandments For Husbands

1. Thou shalt put thy wife before thy mother, thy father, thy daughter, and thy son; for she is thy life long companion.

2. Abuse not thy body with neither excess food, tobacco, or drink, that thy day may be many and healthful in the presence of thy loved ones.

3. Permit neither thy business, nor thy hobby to make a stranger to thy children, for the precious gift a man giveth his family is his time.

4. Forget not the virtue of cleanliness.

5. Make not thy wife a beggar, but share willingly with her thy worldly goods.

6. Forget not to say, "I love you." For even though thy love be constant, the wife doth yearn to hear the words.

7. Remember the approval of thy wife is worth more than the admiring glances of a hundred strangers. Cleave unto her and forsake all others.

8. Keep thy home in good repair, for out of it cometh the joy of thy old age.

9. Forgive with grace, for who among us does not need to be forgiven.

10. Honor thy Lord thy God all the days of thy life, and thy children will rise up and call thee blessed.

Unknown

Ten Commandments For Wives

1. Defile not thy body with excessive foods, tobacco, nor alcohol, that thy days may be long in the house thy husband has provided for thee.

2. Putteth thy husband before thy mother, thy father, thy daughter, and thy son, for he is thy life long companion.

3. Thy shalt not nag.

4. Permit no one to tell thee thou art having a hard time of it; neither thy mother, thy sister, nor thy neighbor, for the Judge will not hold her guiltless who letteth another disparage her husband.

5. Thou shalt not withhold affection from thy husband, for every man loveth to be loved.

6. Forget not the virtue of cleanliness and modest attire.

7. Forgive with grace, for who among us who do not need forgiveness.

8. Remember that the frank approval of thy husband is worth more to thee than the admiring glances of a hundred strangers.

9. Keep thy home in good order, for out of it comes the joys of thy old age.

10. Honor the Lord thy God all the days of thy life, and thy children will rise up and call thee blessed.

Unknown

The Fiftieth Anniversary

Recited at the 50ᵗʰ Wedding Anniversary celebration
for Fred and Betty Grant, November 27, 1993

With heart in throat, I stand to speak:
Spirit is willing, but flesh is weak.
Yet speak I must, for love is strong;
Though voice may falter, heart can't go wrong.

Time passes quickly, a blur it seems
With little thought of important themes
Of life, love, faith, courage, trust . . . .
Yet speak of them today, I must

For these are what we celebrate.
Fifty years ago, a turn of fate
Brought you together, and so began
Your life joined, as woman and man.

The mountain girl and country lad
(Known to us dearly as Mom and Dad)
Began their journey across the land
Heart to heart and hand in hand.

And journey they did, not just in miles,
But also through landscapes of other styles
With roads not marked, paths not lit,
No maps given and no rules writ.

Through these vistas of spirit and soul,
Through joy's great warmth and fear's cruel cold,
Their love's beacon, Heaven's Guide,
Keep them at each others side.

Each trial met was squarely faced
And each blessing with thanksgiving graced.
Through newly wed, parenthood and middle age—
Grandkids too, love carried every stage.

Through all the years, the ups and downs,
With many friends, in many towns
Along the way, for all they've cared,
And with them all, their love they shared.

And for their children, especially,
They've left a glorious legacy,
For the love they taught us, when truly known,
Is a reflection of Heaven's own.

Now hair is grayed and faces lined,
Yet, look within their eyes and find
Love shines there still, so pure, so bright
We cannot fail to see its light.

Their love has brought us here today,
Together to try to find a way
With our laughter and chatter, hugs and kisses too,
To show what's in our hearts—*we* love *you!*

Laura Altevers

"Love shines there still"

Betty and Fred Grant, November 27, 1993
at the celebration of their 50th wedding anniversary

A Red, Red Rose

O my Luve's like a red, red rose,
  That's newly sprung in June:
O my Luve's like the melodie
  That's sweetly play'd in tune!

As fair art thou, my bonnie lass,
  So deep in luve am I;
And I will luve thee still, my dear,
  Till a' the seas gang dry

Till a' the seas gang dry, my dear,
  And the rocks melt wi' the sun;
I will luve thee still, my dear,
While the sands o' life shall run.

And fare thee weel, my only Luve,
  And fare the weel a while!
And I will come again, my Luve,
Tho' it were ten thousand mile.

Robert Burns

In Your Arms

To Grandpa and Grandma
on their 50th Wedding Anniversary (November 27, 1993)

Through many years
Which seem hardly longer than
The span of some tender season,
And across the horizons
Of many mountains and river bottoms,
I have learned one thing:
When I grieve on a bleak night,
You bear me up and carry me.
When I rejoice in life's celebration,
You spin me in a fantastic dance.
When I thunder in strong storm,
You enfold me with a listening heart.
When I long for the fire of your kiss,
You lift me in the garden of paradise.
When I cool the searing desire,
You open up and hold only my hand.
When I work to meet your needs,
You accept it with grateful embrace.
When I stand alone along life's road,
You wipe away the sullen tears.
When I laugh on our brightest morn,
You lift your hands in praise with me.
Whenever, wherever,
These years have taught me,
In your arms, there is my home.

J. Jeremy M. Grant

Betty's grandson, Jeremy Grant

I Look To Thee In Every Need

I looked to Thee in every need,
And never looked in vain—
I feel Thy strong and tender love,
And all is well again.

Samuel Longfellow

Simple Things

The simple things of life are best;
The red sun sinking in the west;
Crisp curtains blowing in the breeze,
The winy fruit from apple trees;
Dim woods with shadows, rank on rank,
Made sleepy by the cowbells clank;
Hills grown silver hid with rain,
A dark night stumbling on his cane;
A heart that laughs, a mind at rest—
Oh simple things of life are best!

Unknown

Work is what you have to do;
Leisure is what you want to do.

George Bernard Shaw

Growing Old

The days grow darker, the nights grow longer;
  The headstones thicken along the way;
And life grows sadder, but love grows stronger
  For those who walk with us day by day.

The tear comes quicker, the laugh comes slower;
  The courage is lesser to do and dare,
And the tide of joy in the heart falls lower,
  And seldom covers the reefs of care.

But all true things in the world seem truer,
  And the better things of earth seem best,
And friends are dearer, as friends are fewer,
  And love is all as our sun dips west.

Then let us clasp hands as we walk together,
  And let us speak softly in love's sweet tone,
For no man knows on the morrow whether
  We two pass on—or but one alone.

Ella Wheeler Wilcox

Touching Shoulders

There's a comforting thought at the close of the day,
When I'm weary and lonely and sad,
That sort of grips hold of my crusty old heart
And bids it be merry and glad.
It gets in my soul and it drives out the blues,
And finally thrills through and through.
It is just a sweet memory that chants the refrain:
"I'm glad I touch shoulders with you!"

Did you know you were brave, did you know you were strong?
Did you know there was one leaning hard?
Did you know that I waited and listened and prayed,
And was cheered by your simplest word?
Did you know that I longed for that smile on your face,
For the sound of your voice ringing true?
Did you know I grew stronger and better because
I had merely touched shoulders with you?

I am glad that l live, that I battle and strive
For the place that I know I must fill;
I am thankful for sorrows, I'll meet with a grin
What fortune may send, good or ill.
I may not have wealth, I may not be great,
But I know I shall always be true,
For I have in my life that courage you gave
When once I rubbed shoulders with you.

Unknown

133

The Tiger

Tiger! Tiger! burning bright,
In the forests of the night,
What immortal hand or eye
Could frame thy fearful symmetry?

In what distant deeps or skies
Burnt the fire of thine eyes?
On what wings dare he aspire?
What the hand dare seize the fire?

And what shoulder, and what art,
Could twist the sinews of thy heart?
And when thy heart began to beat,
What dread hand? and what dread feet?
What the hammer? what the chain?
In what furnace was thy brain?
What the anvil? what dread grasp
Dare its deadly terrors clasp?

When the stars threw down their spears,
And water'd heaven with their tears,
Did He smile his work to see?
Did He who made the Lamb make thee?

Tiger! Tiger! burning bright
In the forests of the night,
What immortal hand or eye
Dare frame thy fearful symmetry?

William Blake

—*Laura Altevers*

An Old Sweetheart Of Mine

An old sweetheart of mine!—
Is this her presence here with me,
Or but a vain creation of a lover's memory?
A fair, illusive vision that would vanish into air
Dared I even touch the silence with the whisper of a prayer?

Nay, let me then believe in all the blended false and
true—
The semblance of the old love and the substance of the new—
The then of changeless sunny days—the now of shower
and shine—
But Love forever smiling—as that old sweetheart of mine.

This ever-restful sense of home, though shouts ring
in the hall—
The easy chair—the old book-shelves and prints
along the wall;
The rare Habanas in their box, or gaunt
church-warden-stem
That often wags, above the jar, derisively at them.

As one who cons at evening o'er an album, all alone,
And muses on the faces of the friends that he has known,
So I turn the leaves of Fancy, till, in shadowy design,
I find the smiling features of an old sweetheart of mine.

The lamplight seems to glimmer with a flicker of surprise,
As I turn it low—to rest me of the dazzle in my eyes,
And light my pipe in silence, save a sigh that seems to yoke
Its fate with my tobacco and to vanish with the smoke.

'Tis a fragrant retrospection—for the loving thoughts
that start
Into being are like perfume from the blossom of the heart;
And to dream the old dreams over is a luxury divine—
When my truant fancies wander with that old
sweetheart of mine.

Though I hear beneath my study, like a fluttering of wings,
The voices of my children and the mother as she sings-
I feel no twinge of conscience to deny me any theme
When Care has cast her anchor in the harbor of a dream-

In fact, to speak in earnest, I believe it adds a charm
To spice the good a trifle with a little dust of harm-
For I find an extra flavor in Memory's mellow wine
That makes me drink the deeper to that old
sweetheart of mine.

O Childhood-days enchanted! O the magic of the Spring!—
With all green boughs to blossom white, and all
bluebirds to sing!
When all the air, to toss and quaff, made life a jubilee
And changed the children's song and laugh to
shrieks of ecstasy.

With eyes half closed in clouds that ooze from lips
that taste, as well,
The peppermint and cinnamon, I hear the old
School bell,
And from "Recess" romp in again from
"Blackman's" broken line,
To smile, behind my "lesson" at that old
sweetheart of mine.

A face of lily beauty, with a form of airy grace,
Floats out of my tobacco as the Genii from the vase;
And I thrill beneath the glances of a pair of azure eyes
As glowing as the summer and as tender as the skies.

I can see the pink sunbonnet and the little checkered dress
She wore when first I kissed her and she answered the
caress
With the written declaration that, "as surely as the vine
Grew 'round the stump," she loved me—that old
sweetheart of mine.

Again I made her presents, in a really helpless way—
The big "Rhode Island Greening"—I was hungry, too,
that day—
But I follow her from Spelling, with her hand behind
her—so—
I slip the apple in it—and the Teacher doesn't know!

I gave my treasures to her—all,—my pencil—blue-and-red;—
And, if little girls played marbles, mine should be all
hers, instead!
But she gave me her photograph, and printed "Ever Thine"
Across the back—in blue-and red—that old
sweetheart of mine.

And again I feel the pressure of her slender little hand,
As we used to talk together of the future we had planned—
When I should be a poet, and with nothing else to do
But write the tender verses that she set the music to . . . .

When we should live together in a cozy little cot
Hid in a nest of roses, with a fairy garden-spot,
Where the vines were ever fruited, and the weather ever fine,
And the birds were ever singing for that old
sweetheart of mine.

———

When I should be her lover forever and a day,
And she my faithful sweetheart till the golden hair was gray;
And we should be so happy that when either's
                    lips were dumb
They would not smile in Heaven till the other's
                    kiss had come.

But, ah! my dream is broken by a step upon the stair;
And the door is softly opened, and—my wife standing there
Yes with eagerness and rapture all my visions I resign—
To greet the living presence of that old sweetheart of mine.

James Whitcomb Riley

Light Shining Out Of Darkness

God moves in a mysterious way,
His wonders to perform;
He plants His footsteps in the sea,
And rides upon the storm.

Deep in unfathomable mines
Of never-failing skill,
He treasures up His bright designs,
And works His sovereign will.

Ye fearful saints, fresh courage take,
The clouds ye so much dread
Are big with mercy, and shall break
In blessings on your head.

Judge not the Lord by feeble sense,
But trust Him for his grace;
Behind a frowning providence,
He hides a smiling face.

His purposes will ripen fast,
Unfolding ev'ry hour;
The bud may have a bitter taste,
But sweet will be the flow'r.

Blind unbelief is sure to err,
And scan his work in vain;
God is His own interpreter,
And He will make it plain.

William Cowper

How The Great Guest Came

Before the cathedral in grandeur rose
At Ingelburg where the Danube goes;
Before its forest of silver spires
Went airily up to the clouds and fires;
Before the oak had ready a beam,
While yet the arch was stone and dream—
There where the altar was later laid,
Conrad, the cobbler, plied his trade.

It happened one day at year's white end—
Two neighbors called on their old-time friend;
They found the shop, so meager and mean,
Made gay with a hundred boughs of green.
Conrad was stitching with face ashine,
But suddenly stopped as he twitched a twine:
"Old friends, good news! At dawn today,
As the cocks were scaring the night away,
The Lord appeared in a dream to me,
And said, 'I am coming your guest to be!'
So I've been busy with feet astir,
Strewing the floor with branches of fir.
The wall is washed and the shelf is shined,
And over the rafter the holly twined.
He comes today, and the table is spread
With milk and honey and wheaten bread."

His friends went home, his face grew still
As he watched for the shadow across the sill.
He lived all the moments o'er and o'er,
When the Lord should enter the lowly door—
The knock, the call, the latch pulled up,
The lighted face, the offered cup,
He would wash the feet where the spikes had been,
He would kiss the hands where the nails went in,
And then at the last would sit with Him
And break the bread as the day grew dim.

While the cobbler mused there passed his pane
A beggar drenched by the driving rain.
He called him in from the stony street
And gave him shoes for his bruised feet.
The beggar went and there came a crone,
Her face with wrinkles of sorrow sown,
A bundle of faggots bowed her back,
And she was spent with the wrench and rack.
He gave her his coat and steadied her load
As she took her way on the weary road.
Then to his door came a little child
Lost and afraid in the world so wild,
In the big, dark world. Catching it up,
He gave it the milk in the waiting cup,
And led it home to its mother's arms,
Out of reach of the world's alarms.

The day went down in the crimson west
And with it the hope of the blessed Guest,
And Conrad sighed as the world turned gray:
"Why is it, Lord, that your feet delay?
Did You forget that this was the day?"
Then soft in the silence a Voice he heard:
"Lift up your heart, for I kept my word.
Three times I came to your friendly door;
Three times my shadow was on your floor.
I was the beggar with bruised feet:
I was the woman you gave to eat;
I was the child on the homeless street!"

Edwin Markham

A Creed

There is a destiny that makes us brothers;
None goes his way alone;
All that we send into the lives of others
Comes back into our own.

I care not what his temples or his creeds,
One thing holds firm and fast—
That into his fateful heap of days and deeds
The soul of man is cast.

Edwin Markham

The Winds Of Fate

One ship drives east and the other drives west
With the selfsame winds that blow,
'Tis the set of the sails
And not the gales
Which tells us the way to go.

Ella Wheeler Wilcox

An Evening Prayer

If I have wounded any soul today,
If I have caused one foot to go astray,
If I have walked in my own willful way—
　　Good Lord, forgive!

If I have uttered idle words or vain,
If I have turned aside from want or pain,
Lest I myself should suffer through the strain—
　　Good Lord, forgive!

If I have cared for joys that are not mine,
If I let my wayward heart repine,
Dwelling on things of earth, not things divine—
　　Good Lord, forgive!

If I have been perverse, or hard, or cold,
If I have longed for shelter in thy fold,
When Thou has given me some part to hold—
　　Good Lord, forgive!

Forgive the sins I confessed to thee,
Forgive the sins I did not see,
That which I know not, Father, teach Thou me—
　　Help me to live.

C. M. Battersby

Man Was Made To Mourn

(Verse 7)

Many and sharp the num'rous ills
Inwoven with our frame!
More pointed still we make ourselves
Regret, remorse, and shame!
And Man, whose heav'n-erected face
The smiles of love adorn,
Man's inhumanity to man
Makes countless thousands mourn!

Robert Burns

He Who Knows

He who knows not, and knows not
that he knows not, is a fool,
shun him;

He who knows not, and knows
that he knows not, is a child,
teach him,

He who knows, and knows not
that he knows, is asleep,
wake him.

He who knows, and knows
that he knows, is wise,
follow him.

Persian Proverb

Retribution

The mills of gods grind late, but they grind fine.

Unknown Greek Poet

Though the mills of God grind slowly,
yet they grind exceedingly small;
Though with patience he stands waiting,
with exactness grinds he all.

F. Von Logau
(Translated by Henry Wadsworth Longfellow)

The Touch Of The Master's Hand

It was battered and scarred, and the auctioneer
Thought it scarcely worth his while
To waste much time on the old violin,
But held it up with a smile:
"What am I bidden, good folks," he cried,
"Who'll start the bidding for me?"
"A dollar, a dollar," then, "Two!" "Only two?
Two dollars, and who'll make it three?
Three dollars, once; three dollars, twice;
Going for three—" But no,
From the room, far back, a gray-haired man
Came forward and picked up the bow;
Then wiping the dust from the old violin,
And tightening the loose strings,
He played a melody pure and sweet
As a caroling angel sings.

The music ceased, and the auctioneer,
With a voice that was quiet and low,
Said, "What am I bid for the old violin?"
And he held it up with the bow.
"A thousand dollars, and who'll make it two
Two thousand! And who'll make it three?
Three thousand, once, three thousand, twice,
And going, and gone," said he.
The people cheered, but some of them cried,
"We do not quite understand
What changed its worth." Swift came the reply:
"The touch of the master's hand."

And many a man with life out of tune,
And battered and scarred with sin,
Is auctioned cheap to the thoughtless crowd,
Much like the old violin.
A "mess of potage," a glass of wine,
A game—and he travels on.
He is "going" once, and "going twice,"
He is "going" and almost "gone."
But the Master comes, and the foolish crowd
Never can quite understand
The worth of a soul and the change that's wrought
By the touch of the Master's hand.

Myra Brooks Welch

More things are wrought by prayer
Than this world dreams of. Wherefore, let thy voice
Rise like a fountain for me night and day.
For what are men better than sheep or goats
That nourish a blind life within the brain,
If knowing God, they lift not hands of prayer
Both for themselves and those who call them friend?

Alfred, Lord Tennyson
(From *Idylls of the King: The Passing of Arthur*)

Abou Ben Adhem

Abou Ben Adhem (may his tribe increase)
Awoke one night from a deep dream of peace,
And saw, within the moonlight in his room,
Making it rich, and like a lily in bloom,
An Angel writing in a book of gold.
Exceeding peace had made Ben Adhem bold,
And to the Presence in the room he said,
"What writest thou?" The Vision raised its head,
And with a look made of all sweet accord
Answered, "The names of those who love the Lord."
"And is mine one?" said Abou. "Nay, not so,"
Replied the angel. Abou spoke more low,
But cheerily still; and said "I pray thee, then,
Write me as one that loves his fellow men."
The Angel wrote, and vanished. The next night
It came again with a great wakening light,
And showed the names whom love of God had blessed,
And, lo, Ben Adhem's name led all the rest!

James Henry Leigh Hunt

The Lord is my shepherd, I shall not want.
He makes me to lie down in green pastures,
he leads me beside still waters, he restores my soul.
He guides me in paths of righteousness
for his name's sake.
Even though I walk through the valley
of the shadow of death,
I will fear no evil, for You are with me;
Your rod and Your staff they comfort me.
You prepare a table before me
in the presence of my enemies.
You anoint my head with oil; my cup overflows.
Surely goodness and mercy will follow me
all the days of my life,
and I will dwell in the house of the Lord forever.

—Psalm 23

The Bible

I Know Not What The Future

I know not what the future hath
Of marvel or surprise,
Assured alone that life and death
His mercy underlies.

And if my heart and flesh are weak
To bear an untried pain,
The bruised reed He will not break
But strengthen and sustain.

And so beside the silent sea
I wait the muffled oar;
No harm from Him can come to me
On ocean or on shore.

I know not where His islands lift
Their fronded palms in airs
I only know I cannot drift
Beyond His love and care.

And Thou, O Lord, by whom are seen
Thy creatures as they be,
Forgive me if too close I lean
My human heart on Thee.

John Greenleaf Whittier
(From *The Eternal Goodness*)

Prayer For Those Who Live Alone

I live alone, dear Lord,
Stay by my side,
In all my daily needs
Be Thou my guide,
Grant me good health,
For that indeed I pray
To carry on my work
From day to day.

Keep pure my mind,
My thoughts, my every deed.
Let me be kind, unselfish
In my neighbors need,
Spare me from fire, from flood,
Malicious tongue,
From thieves, from fear,
And evil ones.

If sickness or accident befall
Then humbly, Lord I pray,
Hear Thou my call.
And when I'm feeling low, or in despair,
Lift up my heart
And help me, is my prayer.
I live alone dear Lord, yet have no fear,
Because I feel your Presence ever near.

AMEN

Unknown

154

Thanatopsis

(Final verse)

So live, that when thy summons comes to join
The innumerable caravan that moves
To that mysterious realm, where each shall take
His chamber in the silent halls of death,
Thou go not, like the quarry-slave at night,
Scourged to his dungeon, but, sustained and soothed
By an unfaltering trust, approach thy grave,
Like one who wraps the drapery of his couch
About him, and lies down to pleasant dreams.

William Cullen Bryant

If we have been joined to Him by dying a death like
His, so we shall be by a resurrection like His.—*Romans 6:5*
The Bible

Crossing The Bar

Sunset and evening star,
And one clear call for me!
And may there be no moaning of the bar,
When I put out to sea.

But such a tide as moving seems asleep,
Too full for sound and foam,
When that which drew from out the boundless deep
Turns again home.

Twilight and evening bell
And after that the dark!
And may there be no sadness of farewell,
When I embark.

For tho' from out our bourne of Time and Place
The flood may bear me far,
I hope to see my Pilot face-to-face
When I have cross'd the bar.

Alfred, Lord Tennyson

Death!

I am a stranger in the land
Where my forefathers trod;
A stranger I unto each heart,
But not unto my God!

I pass along the crowded streets,
Unrecognized my name;
This thought will come amid regrets—
My God is still the same!

I seek with joy my childhood's home,
But strangers claim the sod;
Not knowing where my kindred roam,
Still present is my God!

They tell me my friends all sleep
Beneath the valley clod;
Oh, is not faith submissive sweet!
I have no friend save God!

Unknown

157

There hath not failed one word
of all His good promise.
—*1 Kings 8:59*

Jesus said, "Lo, I am with you always,
even unto the end of the world."
—*Matthew 28:20*

I will never leave thee or forsake thee.
—*Hebrews 13:5*

The Bible

No funeral gloom, my dears, when I am gone . . .
Think of me as withdrawn into the dimness;
Yours still; you mine.
Remember all the best of our past moments
and forget the rest;
And so to where I wait; come gently on.

William Allingham

To A Waterfowl

He, who, from zone to zone,
Guides through the boundless sky thy certain flight,
In the long way that I must tread alone,
Will lead my steps aright.

William Cullen Bryant

—*Marian Wiese*

The quality of mercy is not strained,
It droppeth as the gentle rain from heaven
Upon the place beneath. It is twice blessed,
It blesseth him that gives and him that takes;
'Tis mightiest in the mightiest; it becomes
The throned monarch better than his crown;
His sceptre shows the force of temporal power,
The attribute to awe and majesty,
Wherein doth sit the dread and fear of kings;
But mercy is above this sceptred sway,
It is enthroned in the hearts of kings,
It is an attribute to God himself,
And earthly power doth then show likest Gods
When mercy seasons justice.

William Shakespeare
(From *The Merchant of Venice*)

Meekness is humility, openness to others and to God; willingness to learn; concern for relationships rather than for power; devotion to truth rather than to prestige; trust rather than self assertion. Meekness is necessary for receiving what God wants to give. We receive when we recognize need. We learn when we acknowledge ignorance. We grow in righteousness when we are aware of our sinfulness. We receive power when we understand our helplessness. God is always ready to guide. When we are open to him, we can face with zest the routine of life and we can go calmly and confidently into the unknown.

Unknown

Yesterday is already a dream,
And tomorrow is only a vision;
But today, well lived, makes
Every yesterday a dream of happiness,
And every tomorrow a vision of hope.

From the Sanskrit

The Guy In The Glass

When you get what you want in your struggle for pelf,
    And the world makes you King for a day,
Then go to the mirror and look at yourself,
    And see what that guy has to say.

For it isn't your Father, or Mother, or Wife,
    Who judgment upon you must pass.
The feller whose verdict counts most in your life
    Is the guy staring back from the glass.

He's the feller to please, never mind all the rest,
    For he's with you clear up to the end,
And you've passed your most dangerous, difficult test
    If the guy in the glass is your friend.

You may be like Jack Horner and "chisel" a plum,
    And think you're a wonderful guy,
But the man in the glass says you're only a bum
    If you can't look him straight in the eye.

You can fool the whole world down the pathway of years,
    And get pats on the back as you pass,
But your final reward will be heartaches and tears
    If you've cheated the guy in the glass.

Dale Wimbrow
(Appeared in the *American Magazine* in 1924)

What God Hath Promised

God hath not promised skies always blue,
Flower strewn pathways all our lives thru.
God hath not promised sun without rain,
Joy without sorrow, peace without pain.

God hath not promised we shall not know
Toil and temptation, trouble and woe.
He hath not told us we shall not bear
Many a burden, many a care.

God hath not promised smooth roads and wide,
Swift, easy travel, needing no guide;
Never a mountain rocky and steep,
Never a river turbid and deep.

But God hath promised strength for the day,
Grace for the trials, help from above,
Unfailing sympathy, undying love.

Annie Johnson Flint

My Moment With God

Heavenly Father:
Walk with me today and grant that I may hear
Your footsteps and gladly follow where they lead.
Talk with me today and grant that I may hear
Your tender voice and quicken to its counsel.
Stay with me today and grant that I may feel
Your gentle presence in all that I do and say and think.
Be my strength when I weaken; my courage when I fear.
Help me to know that it is Your hand holding mine
through all the minutes of all the hours of all the day.
And when night folds down, grant that I may know that
I am gathered in Your heart to sleep in love and peace.

AMEN

Unknown

He that dwelleth in the secret place of the most High
shall abide under the shadow of the Almighty.
I shall say of the Lord, He is my refuge and my fortress:
my God, in Him will I trust.
Surely He will deliver thee from the snare of the fowler,
and from the noisome pestilence.
He shall cover thee with his feathers,
and under his wings shall thou trust:
His truth shall be thy shield and buckler.
Thou shalt not be afraid for the terror at night,
or the arrow that flieth by day;
Nor for the pestilence that walketh by night,
nor for the destruction that wasteth at noon day.

—Psalm 91:1-6

The Bible

*(The above prayer and scripture are from
clippings found in Betty's mother's Bible.)*

"I am gathered in Your heart to sleep in love and peace"

Dinksie Lake Robinson, 1884-1971
Betty's mother

Preaching Vs Living

I'd rather see a sermon than hear one any day;
I'd rather one should walk with me than merely tell the way.
The eye's a better pupil and more willing than the ear,
Fine counsel is confusing, but example's always clear;
And the best of all the preachers
are the men who live their creeds,
For to see good put in action is what everybody needs.

I soon can learn to do it if you'll let me see it done;
I can watch your hands in action,
but your tongue too fast may run.
And the lecture you deliver may be very wise and true,
But I'd rather get my lessons by observing what you do;
For I might misunderstand you and the high advise you give,
But there's no misunderstanding
how you act and how you live.

When I see a deed of kindness, I am eager to be kind.
When a weaker brother stumbles
and a strong man stays behind
Just to see if he can help him,
then the wish grows strong in me
To become as big and thoughtful
as I know that friend to be.

And all travelers can witness that the best of guides today
Is not the one who tells them, but the one who shows the way.
One good man teaches many, men believe what they behold;
One deed of kindness noticed is worth forty that are told.
Who stands with men of honor learns to hold his honor dear,
For right living speaks a language which to every one is clear.
Though an able speaker charms me with his eloquence, I say,
I'd rather see a sermon than to hear one, any day.

Edgar A. Guest

The love of reading enables a man to exchange
the wearisome hours of life which comes to everyone
for hours of delight.

Montesquieu

A wise man will hear and increase learning;
And a man of understanding
shall attain into wise counsels.
—*Proverbs. 1:7*

The Bible

Good Morning God

You are ushering in another day
Untouched and freshly new
So here I come to ask You, God,
If you'll renew me, too.
Forgive the many errors
That I made yesterday
And let me try again, dear God,
To walk closer in thy way . . .
But, Father, I am well aware
I can't make it on my own.
So take my hand and hold it tight
For I can't walk alone.

Unknown

Only Believe

Sometimes the road is a long one
And pain walks besides us awhile
Be not afraid, only believe
God's hand is in yours through your trial.
Sometimes the night is a dark one—
The morning seems ages away.
Be not afraid, only believe
He is with you till breaking of day.
And soon comes the brighter tomorrow
Casting aside all that's dim.
He cares for you—be not afraid
Only believe in Him.

Unknown

The Road Not Taken

Two roads diverged in a yellow wood,
And sorry I could not travel both
And be one traveler, long I stood
And looked down one as far as I could
To where it bent in the undergrowth;

Then took the other, as just as fair,
And having perhaps the better claim,
Because it was grassy and wanting wear;
Though as for that, the passing there
Had worn them really about the same.

And both that morning equally lay
In leaves no step had trodden black.
Oh, I kept the first for another day!
Yet knowing how way leads on to way,
I doubted if I should ever come back.

I shall be telling this with a sigh
Somewhere ages and ages hence:
Two roads diverged in a wood, and I—
Took the one less traveled by,
And that has made all the difference.

Robert Frost

If of thy mortal goods thou are bereft
And from thy slender store two loaves
Alone to thee, are left,
Sell one and, with the dole
Buy hyacinths to feed the soul.

Persian Proverb
(Attributed to the Gulistan of Moslih Eddin Saadi,
a Persian poet and Muslim sheik,1184-1291)

Pleasure And Sorrow

I walked a mile with Pleasure,
　She chatted all the way;
But left me none the wiser
　For all she had to say.

I walked a mile with Sorrow,
　And ne'er a word said she.
But oh! The things I learned from her,
　When Sorrow walked with me.

Unknown

Life's Tapestry

My life is but a weaving,
Between my Lord and me;
I cannot choose the colors,
Nor all the pattern see.
Oft times He weaveth sorrow,
And I in foolish pride
Forget He sees the upper
And I the under side.
Nor till the loom is silent
And the shuttle cease to fly.
Shall God unroll the canvass
And explain the reason why
The dark threads are as needful
In the weaver's skillful hand
As the threads of gold and silver
In the pattern He has planned.

Unknown

As A Fond Mother

As a fond mother, when the day is o'er,
Leads by the hand her little child to bed,
Half willing, half reluctant to be led
And leave his broken playthings on the floor,
Still gazing at them through the open door,
Not wholly reassured and comforted
By promises of others in their stead,
Which, though more splendid, may
    not please him more;
So Nature deals with us, and takes away
Our play things one by one, and by the hand
Leads us to rest so gently, that we go
Scarce knowing if we wish to go or stay,
being too full of sleep to understand
How far the unknown transcends
    the what we know.

Henry Wadsworth Longfellow

God shall be my hope, my stay,
My guide, and lantern to my feet.

William Shakespeare

Life gives us blessings without end,
But the greatest of all is the love of a friend.

Unknown

God give you strength for all your needs,
And rest and comfort too—
God bless you with His perfect love,
And grant good health to you.

Unknown

These Are The Gifts I Ask

These are the gifts I ask
Of Thee, Spirit serene,
Strength for the daily task,
Courage to face the road,
Good cheer to help me bear the traveler's load,
And for the hours of rest that come between,
An inward joy of all things heard and seen.

These are the sins I fain
Would have you take away,
Malice and cold disdain,
Hot anger, sullen hate,
Scars of the lonely, envy of the great,
And discontent that casts a shadow gray
On all the brightness of the community.

Henry Van Dyke

Myself

I have to live with myself, and so
I want to be fit for myself to know.
I want to be able, as days go by,
To always look myself in the eye;
I don't want to stand, with the setting sun,
And hate myself for the things I have done.

I can never hide myself from me;
I see what others may never see;
I know what others may never know,
I can never fool myself, and so,
Whatever happens, I want to be
Self-respecting and conscience free.

Edgar A. Guest

The Day Is Done

Some songs have power to quiet
The restless pulse of care,
And come like the benediction
That follows after prayer.

Then read from the treasured volume
The poem of my choice,
And lend to the rhyme of the poet
The beauty of thy voice.

And the night shall be fill'd with music,
And cares that infest the day
Shall fold their tents like the Arabs,
And silently steal away

Henry Wadsworth Longfellow

The Human Touch

'Tis the human touch in this world that counts,
The touch of your hand and mine,
Which means far more to the fainting heart
Than shelter and bread and wine;
For shelter is gone when the night is o'er,
And bread lasts only a day,
But the touch of the hand and the sound of the voice
Sing of the soul always.

Spencer Michael Free

Outwitted

He drew a circle that shut me out—
Heretic, rebel, a thing to flout.
But love and I had the wit to win:
We drew a circle that shut him in.

Edwin Markham

October's Bright Blue Weather

O suns and skies and clouds of June,
And flowers of June together,
Ye cannot rival for one hour
October's bright blue weather.

When loud the bumblebee makes haste,
Belated, thriftless vagrant,
And Golden rod is dying fast,
And lanes with grapes are fragrant.

When Gentians roll their fringes tight,
To save them for the morning,
And chestnuts fall from satin burrs
Without a sound of warning.

When on the ground red apples lie
In piles like jewels shining,
And redder still on the old stone walls
Are leaves of woodbine twining;

When all the lovely wayside things
Their white-winged seeds are sowing,
And in the fields, still green and fair,
Late aftermaths are growing:

When springs run low, and on the brooks,
In idle golden freighting,
Bright leaves sink noiseless in the hush
Of woods, for winter waiting;

When comrades seek sweet country haunts,
By twos and twos together,
And count like misers, hour by hour,
October's bright blue weather.

O suns and skies and flowers of June,
Count all your boasts together,
Love loveth best of all the year
October's bright blue weather.

Helen Hunt Jackson

But as for me, I trust in you, O Lord;
I say, "You are my God,
My times are in your hands."
—*Psalm 31:14-15*

The meek will he guide in judgment;
and the meek will he teach his way.
—*Psalm 25:9*

In thee O Lord, do I put my trust;
Let me never be put to confusion.
—*Psalm 71:1*

As it is written, eye hath not seen, nor ear heard,
neither have entered into the heart of man,
the things which God hath prepared
for them that love Him.
—*1 Corinthians 2:9*

The earth is full of the loving kindness of the Lord.
—*Psalms 33:5*

The Bible

All Things Bright And Beautiful

All things bright and beautiful.
All creatures great and small,
All things wise and wonderful,
The Lord God made them all.

Each little flower that opens,
Each little bird that sings,
He made their glowing colors,
He made their tiny wings.

The purple-headed mountain,
The river running by,
The sunset, and the morning
That brightens up the sky.

The cold wind in the winter,
The pleasant summer sun,
The ripe fruits in the garden,
He made them every one.

The tall trees in the greenwood,
The meadow where we play,
The rushes by the water,
We gather every day.

He gave us eyes to see them,
And lips we might tell
How great is God Almighty,
Who made all things well

Carl Francis Alexander

Barefoot Boy

Blessings on thee, little man,
Barefoot boy, with cheeks of tan!
With thy turned up pantaloons,
And thy merry whistled tunes;
With thy red lip, redder still
Kissed by strawberries on the hill;
With the sunshine on thy face,
Through the torn brim's jaunty grace,
From my heart I give thee joy,—
I was once a barefoot boy!
Prince thou art,—the grown-up man
Only is republican.
Let the million-dollared ride!
Barefoot, trudging at his side,
Thou has more than he can buy
In the reach of ear and eye,—
Outward sunshine, inward joy;
Blessings on thee, barefoot boy!

John Greenleaf Whittier

"Outward sunshine, inward joy"

Fred Grant, Rocky, Oklahoma; 1924

The Sandpiper

Across the lonely beach we flit,
One little sandpiper and I;
And fast I gather, bit by bit,
The scattered driftwood, bleached and dry.
The wild waves reach their hands for it,
The wild wind raves, the tide runs high,
As up and down the beach we flit—
One little sandpiper and I.

Above our heads the sullen clouds
Scud back and forth across the sky;
Like silent ghosts in misty shrouds
Stand out the white lighthouses high,
Almost as far as eye can reach
I see the close-reefed vessels fly,
As fast as we flit along the beach—
One little sandpiper and I.

I watch him as he skims along
Uttering his sweet and mournful cry;
He starts not at my fitful song
Or flash of fluttering drapery.
He has no thought of any wrong,
He scans me with a fearless eye;
Staunch friends are we, well-tried and strong,
The little sandpiper and I.

—

Comrade, where wilt thou be tonight
When the loosed storm breaks furiously?
My driftwood fire will burn so bright
To what warm shelter canst thou fly?
I do not fear for thee, though wroth
The tempest rushes through the sky:
For are we not God's children both,
Thou, little sandpiper, and I?

Celia Thaxter

—Marian Wiese

Old October

Old October's purt' nigh gone,
And the frost is comin' on
A little heavier every day—
Like our hearts is thataway!
Leaves is changin' overhead
Back from green to gray and red,
Brown and yeller, with their stems
Loosenin' on the oaks and e'ms
And the balance of the trees
Gittin' balder every breeze—
Like the heads we're scratchin' on!
Old October's purt' nigh gone.

I love Old October so,
I can't bear to see her go—
Seems to me like losin' some
Old-home relative er chum—
'Pears like sort o' settin' by
Some old friend 'at sigh by sigh
Was a-passin' out o' sight
Into everlastin' night
Hickernuts a feller hears
Rattlin' down is more like tears
Drappin' on the leaves below—
I love Old October so!

Can't tell what it is about
Old October knocks me out!—
I sleep well enough at night—
And the blamest appetite
Ever mortal man possessed,—
Last thing et, it tastes the best!—
Walnuts, butternuts, pawpaws,
'Iles and limbers up my jaws
Fer real service, sich as new
Pork, spareribs, and sausage, too.—
Yit, fer all, they's somepin' 'bout
Old October knocks me out!

James Whitcomb Riley

To My Dear And Loving Husband

If ever two were one, then surely we.
If ever man were loved by wife, then thee;
If ever wife were happy in a man,
Compare with me, ye woman, if you can.
I prize my love more than whole mines of gold,
Of all the riches that the East doth hold.
My love is such that rivers cannot quench,
Nor aught but love from thee, give recompense.
Thy love is such I can no way repay,
The heavens reward the manifold, I pray.
Then while we live, in love let's so persevere
That when we live no more, we may live ever.

Anne Bradstreet

"If ever two were one"

Fred and Betty Grant

The Old Swimmin'-Hole

Oh! The old swimmin'-hole! whare the crick so still and deep
   Looked like a baby-river that was laying half asleep,
And the gurgle of the worter round the drift jest below
Sounded like the laugh of something we onc't ust to know
   Before we could remember anything but the eyes
     Of the angels lookin' out as we left Paradise;
   But the merry days of youth is beyond our controle,
And it's hard to part ferever with the old swimmin'-hole.

Oh! the old swimmin'-hole! In the happy days of yore,
   When I ust to lean above it on the old sickamore,
   Oh! it showed me a face in its warm sunny tide
    That gazed back at me so gay and glorified,
   It made me love myself, as I leaped to caress
My shadder smilin' up at me with sich tenderness.
But them days is past and gone, and old Time's tuck his toll
From the old man come back to the old swimmin'-hole.

   Oh! the old swimmin'-hole! In the long lazy days
When the humdrum of school made so many run-a-ways,
   How plesant was the jurney down the old dusty lane,
Whare the tracks of our bare feet was all printed so plane
   You could tell by the dent of the heel and the sole
They was lots o' fun on hands at the old swimmin'-hole.
   But the lost joys is past! Let your tears in sorrow roll
Like the rain that ust to dapple up the old swimmin'-hole.

—

Thare the bullrushes growed, and the cattails so tall,
And the sunshine and shadder fell over it all;
And it mottled the worter with amber and gold
Tel the glad lilies rocked in the ripples that rolled;
And the snake-feeder's four gauzy wings fluttered by
Like the ghost of a daisy dropped out of the sky,
Or a wownded apple-blossom in the breeze's controle
As it cut acrost some orchard to'rds the old swimmin'-hole.

Oh! the old swimmin'-hole! When I last saw the place,
The scene was all changed, like the change in my face;
The bridge of the railroad now crosses the spot
Where the old divin'-log lays sunk and fergot.
And I stray down the banks whare the trees used to be—
But never again will theyr shade shelter me!
And I wish in my sorrow I could strip to the soul,
And dive off in my grave like the old swimmin'-hole.

James Whitcomb Riley

Jenny Kiss'd Me

Jenny kiss'd me when we met,
Jumping from the chair she sat in;
Time you thief, who love to get
Sweets into your list, put that in!
Say I'm weary, say I'm sad,
Say that health and wealth have miss'd me,
Say I'm growing old, but add,
Jenny kiss'd me.

James Henry Leigh Hunt

Trees

I think I shall never see
A poem lovely as a tree.

A tree whose hungry mouth is prest
Against the earth's sweet flowing breast;

A tree that looks at God all day,
And lifts her leafy arms to pray;

A tree that may in Summer wear
A nest of robins in her hair;

Upon whose bosom snow has lain;
Who intimately lives with rain.

Poems are made by fools like me,
But only God can make a tree.

Joyce Kilmer

—*Marian Wiese*

When The Frost Is On The Punkin

When the frost is on the punkin and the fodder's in the shock,
    And you hear the kyouck and gobble of the
                struttin' turkey-cock,
And the clackin' of the guineys, and the cluckin' of the hens,
And the rooster's hallylooyer as he tiptoes on the fence;
    O, it's then's the times a feller is a-feelin' at his best,
    With the risin' sun to greet him from a night of
                peaceful rest,
        As he leaves the house, bareheaded, and goes out
                to feed the stock,
        When the frost is on the punkin and the fodder's
                in the shock.

They's something kindo' harty-like about the atmusfere
When the heat of summer's over and the coolin' fall is here—
    Of course we miss the flowers, and the blossums
                on the trees,
    And the mumble of the hummin' birds and the
                buzzin' of the bees;
        But the air's so appetizin'; and the landscape
                through the haze
Of a crisp and sunny morning of the airly autumn days
    Is a pictur' that no painter has the colorin' to mock—
        When the frost is on the punkin and the fodder's
                in the shock.

The husky, rusty russel of the tossels of the corn,
And the raspin' of the tangled leaves, as golden as the morn;
The stubble in the furries—kindo' lonesome-like, but still
A-preachin' sermons to us of the barns they
growed to fill;
The strawstack in the medder, and the reaper in the shed;
The hosses in theyr stalls below—the clover overhead!—
O, it sets my hart a-clickin' like the tickin' of a clock,
When the frost is on the punkin and the fodder's
in the shock!

Then your apples all is gethered, and the ones a feller keeps
Is poured around the celler-floor in red and yeller heaps;
And your cider-makin's over, and your
wimmern-folks is through
With their mince and apple butter, and theyr souse
and sausage, too! . . .
I don't know how to tell it—but ef sich a thing could be
As the Angels wantin' boardin', and they'd call
around on me—
I'd want to 'commodate 'em—all the whole-indurin' flock—
When the frost is on the punkin and the fodder's
in the shock!

James Whitcomb Riley

—Marian Wiese

Daffodils

I wandered lonely as a cloud
That floats on high o'er vales and hills,
When all at once I saw a crowd—
A host of golden daffodils
Beside the lake, beneath the trees,
Fluttering and dancing in the breeze.

Continuous as the stars that shine
And twinkle on the Milky Way,
They stretched in never-ending line
Along the margin of the bay:
Ten thousand saw I at a glance,
Tossing their heads in sprightly dance.

The waves beside them danced, but they
Out did the sparkling waves in glee;
A poet could not but be gay
In such a jocund company;
I gazed—and gazed—but little thought
What wealth the show to me had brought.

For oft, when on my couch I lie,
In vacant or in pensive mood,
They flash upon my inward eye
Which is the bliss of solitude;
And then my heart with pleasure fills,
And dances with the daffodils.

William Wordsworth

The First Snowfall

The snow had begun in the gloaming
And busily all the night
Had been heaping field and highway
With silence deep and white.

Even pine and fir and hemlock
Wore ermine too dear for an earl,
And the poorest twig on the elm-tree
Was ridged inch deep with pearl.

From sheds new-roofed with Carrara
Came Chanticleer's muffled crow,
The stiff rails were softened with swan's-down
And still fluttered down the snow.

I stood and watched by the window
The noiseless work of the sky,
And the sudden flurries of snow-birds,
Like brown leaves whirling by.

I thought of a mound in sweet Auburn
Where a little headstone stood;
How the flakes were folding it gently,
As did robins the babes in the wood.

Up spoke our own little Mabel,
Saying, "Father, who makes it snow?"
And I told of the good All-father
Who cares for us here below.

Again I looked at the snow-fall,
And thought of the leaden sky
That arched o'er our first great sorrow,
When that mound was heaped so high.

I remembered the gradual patience
That fell from that cloud-like snow,
Flake by flake, healing and hiding
The scar of our deep-plunged woe.

And again to the child I whispered,
"The snow that husheth all,
Darling, the merciful Father
Alone can make it fall."

Then, with eyes that saw not, I kissed her;
And she, kissing back, could not know
That my kiss was given to her sister,
Folded close under deepening snow.

James Russell Lowell

The Bridge

I stood on the bridge at midnight,
As the clocks were striking the hour,
And the moon rose o'er the city,
Behind the dark clock tower.

I saw her bright reflection
In the water under me,
Like a golden goblet falling
And sinking into the sea.

And far in the hazy distance
Of that lovely night in June,
The blaze of the flaming furnace
Gleamed redder than the moon.

Among the long, black rafters
The wavering shadows lay,
And the current that came from the ocean
Seemed to lift and bear them away;

As, sweeping and eddying through them,
Rose the belated tide,
And, streaming into the moonlight,
The seaweed floated wide.

And like those waters rushing
Among the wooden piers,
A flood of thoughts came o'er me
That filled my eyes with tears.

How often, oh how often,
In the days that had gone by,
I had stood on that bridge at midnight
And gazed on that wave and sky!

How often, oh how often,
I had wished that the ebbing tide
Would bear me away on its bosom
O'er the ocean wild and wide!

For my heart was hot and restless,
And my life was full of care,
And the burden laid upon me
Seemed greater than I could bear.

But now it has fallen from me,
It is buried in the sea;
And only the sorrow of others
Throws its shadow over me.

Yet whenever I cross the rivers
On its bridge with wooden piers
Like the odor of brine from the ocean
Comes the thought of other years.

And I think how many thousands
Of care-encumbered men,
Each bearing his burden of sorrow,
Have crossed the bridge since then.

I see the long procession
Still passing to and fro,
The young heart hot and restless,
And the old subdued and slow!

———

And forever and forever,
As long as the river flows,
As long as the heart has passions,
As long as life has woes;

The moon and its broken reflection
And its shadows shall appear,
As the symbol of love in heaven,
And its wavering image here.

Henry Wadsworth Longfellow

If I can stop one heart from breaking,
I shall not live in vain,
If I can ease one life the aching,
Or cool one pain,
Or help one fainting robin
Into his nest again,
I shall not live in vain.

Emily Dickinson
(From *Complete Poems—Life: Verse 6*)

The Beautiful Life

When you go out in the morning
To begin the work of the day,
Don't neglect the little chances
You find along your way;
For in lifting another's burden,
And speaking a word of cheer;
You will find your own cares lighter,
And easier for you to bear.

Forget each kindness that you do
As soon as you have done it;
Forget the praise that falls to you
The moment you have won it.
Forget the slander that you hear
Before you can repeat it
Forget each slight, each spite, each sneer
Wherever you may meet it.

Remember every kindness done
To you whate'er its measure;
Remember praise by others won,
And pass it on with pleasure;
Remember every promise made,
And keep it to the letter,
Remember those who lent you aid,
And be a grateful debtor.

Unknown

The Year's At The Spring

The year's at the spring
And the day's at the morn;
Morning's at seven;
The hillside's dew-pearled;
The lark's on the wing;
The snail's on the thorn:
God's in his heaven—
All's right with the world!

Robert Browning

Our Lips And Ears

If your lips would keep from slips,
Five things observe with care;
Of whom you speak, to whom you speak,
And how and when and where.
If your ears would save from jeers,
These things keep meekly hid:
Myself and I, and mine and my,
And how I do and did.

Unknown

A Backward Look

As I sat smoking, alone, yesterday,
And lazily leaning back in my chair,
Enjoying myself in a general way—
Allowing my thoughts a holiday
From weariness, toil and care—
My fancies—doubtless, for ventilation—
Left ajar the gates of my mind—
And Memory, seeing the situation,
Slipped out on the street of "Auld Lang Syne"—

Wandering ever with tireless feet
Through scenes of silence, and jubilee
Of long-hushed voices; and faces sweet
As far as the eye could see;
Dreaming again, in anticipation,
The same old dreams of our boyhood's days
That never come true, from the vague sensation
Of walking asleep in the world's strange ways.

Away to the house where I was born!
And there was the selfsame clock that ticked
From the close of dusk to the burst of morn,
When life-warm hands plucked the golden corn
And helped when the apples were picked.
And the "chiny dog" on the mantel-shelf,
With the gilded collar and yellow eyes,
Looked just as at first, when I hugged myself
Sound asleep with the dear surprise.

And down to the swing in the locust-tree,
Where the grass was worn from the trampled ground,
And where "Eck" Skinner, "Old" Carr and three
    Or four such other boys used to be
    "Doin' sky-scrapers," or "whirlin' round":
And again Bob climbed for the bluebird's nest,
And again "had shows" in the buggy-shed
Of Guymon's barn, where still, unguessed,
The old ghosts romp through the best days dead!

And again I gazed from the old schoolroom
    With a wistful look, of a long June day,
When on my cheek was the hectic bloom
    Caught at Mischief, as I presume—
        He had such a "partial" way
It seemed toward me—And again I thought
    Of a probable likelihood to be
Kept in after school—for a girl was caught
    Catching a note from me.

And down through the woods to the swimming hole—
Where the big, white, hollow old sycamore grows—
    And we never cared when the water was cold,
    And always "ducked" the boy that told
        On the fellow that tied the clothes—
When life went so like a dreamy rhyme,
    That it seems to me now that then
The world was having a jollier time
    Than it will ever have again.

James Whitcomb Riley

The House By The Side Of The Road

There are hermit souls that live withdrawn
In the peace of their self-content,
There are souls, like stars, that dwell apart
In a fellowless firmament;
There are pioneer souls that blaze their paths
Where highways never ran,
But let me live by the side of the road
And be a friend to man.

Let me live in a house by the side of the road
Where the race of men go by—
The men who are good and the men who are bad
As good and as bad as I.
I would not sit in the scorner's seat,
Or hurl the cynic's ban,
Let me live in the house by the side of the road
And be a friend to man.

I see from my house by the side of the road,
By the side of the highway of life,
The men who press with ardor of hope,
The men who are faint with the strife,
But I turn not away from their smiles nor their tears—
Both parts of an infinite plan,
Let me live in a house by the side of the road
And be a friend to man.

Let me live in a house by the side of the road
Where the race of men go by—
They are good, they are bad, they are weak, they are strong.
Wise, foolish—so am I.
Then why should I sit in the scorner's seat
Or hurl the cynic's ban?—
Let me live in the house by the side of the road
And be a friend to man.

Sam Walter Foss

"A house by the side of the road"

Home of John W. and Elizabeth Lakes,
Betty's grandparents, in Berea, Kentucky

Do Not Go Gentle Into That Good Night

Do not go gentle into that good night,
Old age should burn and rave at close of day;
Rage, rage against the dying of the light.

Though wise men at their end know dark is right,
Because their words had forked no lightening they
Do not go gentle into that good night.

Good men, the last wave by, crying how bright
Their frail deeds might have danced in a green bay,
Rage, rage against the dying of the light.

Wild men who caught and sang the sun in flight,
And learn, to late, they grieved it on its way,
Do not go gentle into that good night.

Grave men, near death, who see with blinding light
Blind eyes could blaze like meteors and be gay,
Rage, rage against the dying of the light.

And you my father, there on the sad height,
Curse, bless, me now with your fierce tears, I pray.
Do not go gentle into that good night,
Rage, rage against the dying of the light.

By Dylan Thomas from the POEMS OF DYLAN THOMAS copyright ©1952 by Daylan Thomas. Reprinted by permission of New Directions Publishing Corp.

Elegy In A Country Church Yard

The curfew tolls the knell of parting day,
The lowing herd winds slowly o'er the lea,
The plowman homeward plods his weary way,
And leaves the world to darkness and to me.

Now fades the glimmering landscape on the sight,
And all the air a solemn stillness holds,
Save where the beetle wheels his droning flight,
And drowsy tinklings lull the distant folds;

Save that from yonder ivy-mantled tower,
Where the moping owl does to the moon complain,
Of such as, wandering near her secret bower,
Molest her ancient solitary reign.

Beneath those rugged elms, that yew tree's shade,
Where heaves the turf in many a moldering heap,
Each in his narrow cell forever laid,
The rude forefathers of the hamlet sleep.

The breezy call of incense-breathing morn,
The swallow twittering from the straw-built shed,
The cock's shrill clarion, the echoing horn,
No more shall rouse them from their lowly bed.

For them no more the blazing hearth shall burn,
Nor busy housewife ply her evening care;
No children run to greet their sire's return
Or climb his knee the envied kiss to share.

Oft did the harvest to their sickle yield,
Their furrow oft the stubborn glebe has broke;
How jocund did they drive their team afield!
How bowed the woods beneath their sturdy stroke!

Let not Ambition mock their useful toil,
Their homely joys, and destiny obscure;
Nor Grandeur hear with disdainful smile
The short and simple annals of the poor.

The boast of heraldry, the pomp of pow'r,
And all that beauty, all that wealth e'er gave,
Await alike the inevitable hour;
The paths of glory lead but to the grave.

Nor you, ye proud, impute to these the fault,
If Memory o'er their tomb no trophies raise,
Where, through the long-drawn aisle and fretted vault,
The pealing anthem swells the note of praise.

Can storied urn, or animated bust,
Back to it's mansion call the fleeting breath?
Can Honor's voice provoke the silent dust,
Or Flattery soothe the dull, cold ear of Death?

Perhaps in this neglected spot is laid
Some heart once pregnant with celestial fire;
Hands that the rod of empire might have swayed,
Or wake to ecstasy the living lyre;

But Knowledge to their eyes her ample page,
Rich with the spoils of time, did ne'er unroll;
Chill penury repressed their noble rage,
And froze the genial current of the soul.

Full many a gem of purest ray serene,
The dark unfathomed caves of ocean bear;
Full many a flower is born to blush unseen,
And waste its sweetness on the desert air.

Some village-Hampden, that, with dauntless breast,
The little tyrant of his fields withstood,
Some mute, inglorious Milton here may rest,
Some Cromwell, guiltless of his country's blood.

The applause of list'ning senates to command,
The threats of pain and ruin to despise,
To scatter plenty o'er a smiling land,
And read their history in a nation's eyes.

Their lot forbad: nor, circumscribed alone
Their growing virtues, but their crimes confined;
Forbad to wade through slaughter to a throne,
And shut the gates of Mercy on mankind,

The struggling pangs of concious truth to hide,
To quench the blushes of ingenuous shame,
Or heap the shrine of Luxury and Pride
With incense kindled at the Muse's flame.

Far from the madding crowd's ignoble strife
Their sober wishes never learned to stray;
Along the cool sequestered vale of life
They kept the noiseless tenor of their way.

Yet ev'n these bones from insult to protect
Some frail memorial still erected nigh,
With uncouth rhymes and shapeless sculpture decked,
Implores the passing tribute of a sigh.

Their name, their years, spelt by th' unlettered Muse,
    The place of fame and elegy supply:
    And many a holy text around she strews,
    That teach the rustic moralist to die.

    For who, to dumb Forgetfulness a prey,
    This pleasing anxious being e'er resigned,
    Left the warm precincts of the cheerful day,
    Nor cast one longing ling'ring look behind?

    On some fond breast the parting soul relies,
    Some pious drops the closing eye requires;
    Ev'n from the tomb the voice of Nature cries,
    Ev'n in our ashes live their wonted fires.

For thee, who, mindful of th' unhonoured dead,
    Dost in these lines their artless tale relate;
    If chance, by lonely Contemplation led,
    Some kindred spirit shall enquire thy fate,—

    Haply some hoary-headed swain may say
    "Oft have we seen him at the peep of dawn
    Brushing with hasty steps the dews away
    To meet the sun upon the upland lawn;

    "There at the foot of yonder nodding beech,
    That wreathes its old fantastic roots so high,
His listless length at noon-tide would he stretch,
    And pore upon the brook that babbles by.

    "Hard by yon wood, now smiling as in scorn,
    Mutt'ring his wayward fancies would he rove;
    Now drooping, woeful-wan, like one forlorn,
Or crazed with care, or crossed in hopeless love.

———

"One morn I missed him from the customed hill,
Along the heath, and near his fav'rite tree;
Another came; nor yet beside the rill,
Nor up the lawn, nor at the wood was he:

"The next, with dirges due in sad array
Slow through the church-way path we saw him borne.
Approach and read, for thou can'st read, the lay
Graved on the stone beneath yon aged thorn."

The Epitaph

Here rests his head upon the lap of earth
A Youth, to Fortune and to Fame unknown:
Fair Science frowned not on his humble birth,
And Melancholy marked him for her own.

Large was his bounty, and his soul sincere,
Heaven did a recompense as largely send:
He gave to Misery (all he had) a tear,
He gained from Heaven ('twas all he wished) a friend.

No farther seek his merits to disclose,
Or draw his frailties from their dread abode,
(There they alike in trembling hope repose,)
The bosom of his Father and his God.

Thomas Gray

"Each in his narrow cell forever laid"

Highland Cemetery, Highland County, Ohio
The gravestone of Malinda McPherson Haynes
(1853–1890), grandmother of Fred Grant,
is in the front left corner of this photo

To A Louse

O wad some power the giftie gie us
To see oursel's as ithers see us!
It wad frae monie a blunder free us
And foolish notion:
What airs in dress an' gait wad lea'e us,
And ev'n devotion!

Robert Burns

A Wise Old Owl

A wise old owl lived in an oak,
The more he saw the less he spoke;
The less he spoke the more he heard:
Why can't we all be like that wise old bird?

Edward Hersey Richards

O Captain! My Captain!

O Captain! my Captain! our fearful trip is done,
The ship has weathered every rack,
the prize we sought is won,
The port is near, the bells I hear, the people all
exulting,
While follow eyes the steady keel, the vessel grim and
daring;
But O heart! heart! heart!
O bleeding drops of red,
Where on the deck my Captain lies
Fallen cold and dead.

O Captain! my Captain! rise up and hear the bells;
Rise up—for you the flag is flung—for you the bugle
trills,
For you bouquets and ribbon'd wreaths—
for you the shores a-crowding,
For you they call, the swaying mass, their eager faces
turning;
Here Captain! dear father!
This arm beneath your head
It is some dream that on the deck,
You've fallen cold and dead.

My Captain does not answer, his lips are pale and still,
My father does not feel my arm, he has no pulse or will,
The ship is anchored safe and sound,
its voyage closed and done,
From fearful trip the victor ship comes in with object
won:
Exult O shores, and ring O bells;
But I with mournful tread,
Walk the deck my Captain lies,
Fallen cold and dead.

Walt Whitman

Index of Authors

Adams, S.; Baer, A.; Meyer, G.W 105
Alexander, Carl Francis 184
Allingham, William 158
Allison, Joy 31
Altevers, Laura 125
Arabian Proverb 90
Battersby, C. M. 145
Bible, The 50, 95, 152, 155, 158, 165, 168, 183
Blake, William 134
Bradstreet, Anne 191
Brine, Mary Dow 29
Browning, Robert 206
Bryant, William Cullen 155, 159
Bryon, Eva 102
Burns, Robert 128, 146, 218
Clow, Dr. Hollis E. 55
Cowper, William 140
David, M.; Kent, W. 105
Dickinson, Emily 204
Dromgoole, William Allan 92
Fields, Eugene 80, 82
Fletcher, Julia A. 48
Flint, Annie Johnson 93, 163
Foss, Sam Walter 209
Free, Spencer Michael 180
Frost, Robert 171
Gillilan, Strickland 38
Grant, Betty Robinson 109
Grant, J. Jeremy M. 129
Gray, Thomas 212

Guest, Edgar A. 167, 178
Heyliger, Fleur Conkling 48
Hood, Thomas 19
Hunt, James Henry Leigh 151, 195
Jackson, Helen Hunt 181
Kilmer, Joyce 196
Lathrap, Mary Torrans 108
Lee, Agnes 27
Lincoln, Abraham 21
Logau, F. Von 148
Longfellow, Henry W. 51, 56, 175, 179, 202
Longfellow, Samuel 131
Lovelace, Richard 89
Lowell, James Russell 117, 200
MacDonald, George 42, 101
Markham, Edwin 36, 141, 143, 180
McRae, John 24
Milnes, Richard M., Lord Houghton 106
Montesquieu 168
Mulligan, James H. 25
Murray, Wm. H. H. 98
Niebuhr, Rheinhold 90
Parry, Joseph 85
Persian Proverb 147, 172
Richards, Edward Hersey 218
Riley, James Whitcomb 60, 65, 68, 71, 76, 136, 189, 193, 197, 207
Sangster, Margaret 87
From the Sanskrit 161
Schultz, Samantha 46
Selected Sayings 55
Shakespeare, William 160, 176
Shaw, George Bernard 131
Stevenson, Robert Lewis 54, 59
Tanksley, Peter 96
Tennyson, Alfred Lord 150, 156
Thaxter, Celia 187
Thomas, Dylan 211

Unknown 40, 49, 50, 79, 86, 88, 91, 94, 97, 110, 121, 123, 131, 133,
    148, 154, 157, 161, 164, 169, 170, 173, 174, 176, 205, 206
Van Dyke, Henry 177
Wagstaff, Blanche S. 103
Welch, Myra Brooks 149
Wesley, John 99
Whitman, Walt 219
Whittier, John Greenleaf 32, 112, 153, 185
Wilcox, Ella Wheeler 35, 132, 144
Wimbrow, Dale 162
Wordsworth, William 64, 100, 119
World War II Song 105